Dorothy
Never Got
Down Like This

ERIN HUNSADER

For the dreamers who aren't afraid to

chase their dreams.

To Mom and Nana - the two strong ladies

who made my journey possible.

Introduction

Once upon a time there was a girl. She was tall, gangly, and awkward, like a baby ostrich learning to walk. She was shy, quiet, and a middle child, which is a polite way to say *messed up*. And, by the way, she's me - Erin Hunsader.

You don't know me, so let's set my narrative in the framework of a person you might know. The beloved character of Dorothy from *The Wizard of Oz*, written by the fabulous L. Frank Baum, to pay homage to the character. Truthfully, I've always felt a little like her; naïve, misunderstood. Someone who wants to be heard. Isn't that what we all want? To be heard?

And while I can relate to Dorothy, my journey ahead wasn't similar to hers at all. She made it safely out of Oz and back home while in a dream. My journey was a story of failure – or so I thought. In that presumed failure, I found the answers I was looking for. I hope you enjoy my story of chasing my dream to become a musical theatre writer on Broadway and how I risked it all.

Chapter One

Follow Your Yellow Brick Road

Dorothy grew up in Kansas. I grew up in a tiny town in another Midwestern state. I was born on a hot summer day in Sturgeon Bay, Wisconsin. Nothing like naming a town after a really ugly fish.

Sturgeon Bay is set at the mouth of the Door County Peninsula, so we essentially lived on an island. Because of this, my father was big on teaching me and my siblings to swim from birth. He wasn't passive about plopping us into the water along with our family dog and seeing which one of us would sink first. I'm kidding, it wasn't that bad - he would usually save the dog.

My parents are polar opposites - my mother is an artist and painter and my father, well, the best way to describe him is angry.

Why is that with dads? It's like they devolve from fully formed speaking individuals when dating to guys who grunt, fart, and burp after marriage. I have two brothers who are polar opposites, too, which makes for interesting family get-togethers.

I grew up Catholic, going to the local Catholic church, attending Catholic school. Because we lived in a small town, the Catholic school was a reflection of that. My first five years of school were spent with the same handful of kids, not to mention the same handful of nuns for teachers. I remember the first time I saw the movie, *The Wizard of Oz* I thought Miss Gulch was one of the nuns at school. Probably because I'd seen a nun toss a kid down a flight of stairs while he was still seated in his desk, jab a kid in the crotch with a pencil, and verbally terrorize a child to the point of him becoming comatose. Oh, those great Catholic school memories.

Thank God I had a great aunt who was a nun and happened to be the loveliest lady in the world. All the other nuns knew and liked her, which gave me a sort of immunity. If one of the nuns tried to lay a hand on me, I would smile and say, "Sister Madonna knows you."

Then, they'd snap out of their psychotic state and smile back at me.

My brothers didn't have as much luck. I think the nuns had it out for the boys.

In 6th grade, I begged my mom to let me go to public school. She agreed, and I blossomed. I found, much like my love of New York, that going somewhere larger, with a more diverse population was the best thing for me. I was able to be exactly who I wanted to be, and nobody cared. My grades got better, and soon, I was on the honor roll. I made new friends, and even made it onto the student council. But more than that, it seemed for the first time that I didn't have to try as hard. Times like that are incredible gifts - when everything is falling into place naturally. I try to recognize those moments because they're rare.

Door County, where I grew up, is a peaceful area. My parents could never figure out where I developed an obsession with New York City. My father thinks Sturgeon Bay (population: 10,001) is too busy and my mother gets nervous

   Dorothy Never Got Down Like This

driving to Green Bay (population: 105,139), so a metropolitan city like New York City seemed a rather abnormal interest for me.

I'm a text book middle child though, which one can describe as: insecure, has feelings of never fitting in, always does things for attention, and has interest in the arts. Of course, looking outward from the little burb of a town we lived in made sense to me. New York seemed like a place where I would finally fit in. New York became a character to me all its own, almost like a person I'd met who'd become my best friend. Yes, I was obsessed.

Somehow this obsession became my identity, and my family loved to tease me about it. People would buy me gifts adorned with images of New York, which was all well and good. The obsession seemed innocent enough. There was just one problem - I'd never been there.

My dad never liked crowds or going anywhere that had a population. He never said, "Hey kids, let's go to Disney Land!"

No, my father's idea of *getting away* was loading us all into the car and taking us to Dairy Queen. The trips to Dairy Queen usually ended with one of us kids laughing too loud and then dropping the swirl off of our ice cream cone in the backseat of the car.

This caused Dad to lose his shit and speed out of the parking lot, cursing at us the whole way home. My younger brother would start crying and Mom would yell at my father about how much it cost to take the entire family out for ice cream (or ice milk – whatever they serve at DQ). Then my older brother would lean over to me and say, "Why are our parents so crazy?"

Despite his impatience, my father did enjoy the outdoors. My mother, however, did not. Mushroom picking in the woods was our other summer excursion - imagine the fun!

No. It was miserable, especially after my father ate a bad mushroom - something my mother had predicted. He threw up for three days and we all thought he was going to die. After thinking he might be dying, that put the kibosh on the mushroom picking outings.

By the time I was sixteen, the farthest I'd ever been from Wisconsin was when I visited Minnesota with my grandparents. The landscape is relatively the same as Wisconsin's, just a little colder. *Great!*

I was beginning to feel as if I'd never see the Big Apple, but something within me knew it would happen. I couldn't give up on my dream. I didn't know how or when. I just knew there would be a moment when the universe would align and tell me, "Hey Erin, here's your chance."

Which is exactly what happened.

Okay, not really. But close.

A little luck and a lot of begging went into planning a visit to New York. My grandparents were classy people. Thank heavens for that, because God knows, my family and I weren't. Screaming at each other in our rusted-out car in the Dairy Queen parking lot had never impressed the elites of Sturgeon Bay, go figure.

My grandparents loved to travel, planning trips to Hawaii, Florida, Arizona - mostly warm places. I never suspected they'd ever want to venture out and visit New York City.

It was a month before my sixteenth birthday when I heard my grandparents talking with my parents outside on the deck. They were discussing their latest plans for a trip to NYC.

WHAT?

I ran from my room and out the patio door in such a flurry I nearly crashed through the screen door. I'm naturally clumsy so nobody was surprised.

My grandfather looked up from his martini and smiled at me.

I have to segue here. My grandfather was a judge for a long time in our tiny town. This may explain why nobody wanted to date me in high school. Or it could have been my lack of social skills and the fact that I was a head taller than all of the boys, but who's to say. I loved going places with my grandparents because, as in any small town, everybody knows everybody. People would greet him by saying, "Hello, your Honor."

Your Honor. How cool is that?

And he was honorable. He was statuesque with an intimidating presence. The one thing I remember most about my grandfather was his ability to help people see the best in themselves and go on to develop those qualities.

Oh sure, he would tease me and my brothers about little things, but he was always there to let us know what was unique about each one of us. He'd explain to us how we could enhance those qualities, too.

I knew he was aware of my obsession with New York, so when I stepped outside and asked them what they were talking about, he was one step ahead of me.

"We're taking a trip to New York City," Bubba said. (Yes, we called our distinguished grandfather Bubba.)

"Really, New York City?" I asked as calmly as I could, totally freaking out on the inside.

"I'm going, too," Mom said, ecstatic.

I stood there for a moment waiting for the other shoe to drop, but it didn't.

"And me?" I asked. "You're taking me, too? I love New York City. I'm dying to go to New York City. You all know I'm obsessed with New York City!"

Being almost sixteen, I couldn't contain my excitement.

"Erin, go in the house," Mom said.

My head sank to my chest and I went inside, defeated.

I turned on the TV and laid down on the living room floor, staring up at the ceiling. *How could they go to New York City and not take me?*

It must have been nine o'clock when my grandparents left that night. Mom came inside and saw me still lying in that same spot. I heard her sigh as she headed toward the kitchen. Not wanting to talk to anyone, I got up and went to my bedroom.

The next few days I tried to keep my thoughts off of that conversation we had on the deck. Mom asked me if I was okay. I said I was fine, but she knew I wasn't. I didn't want to whine about it. My Grandparents had made their decision and who was I to intrude on their trip.

Then one night later that week, Mom came into my

bedroom while I was hanging up my clothes. She sat on my bed, silent.

"I don't want to talk about it," I said, assuming she was going to go into a diatribe about how I needed to get over it and be grateful for what I had…blah, blah, blah.

"I talked to Nana and Bubba," she said, "and they thought it would be nice if…if you could come with us, too."

I held my breath.

"It's going to be your birthday and Christmas gifts this year from them, just so you know."

I threw my laundry into the air with ebullience. "I don't care, I don't care. Oh my God, thank you, Mom!" I hugged her tight and thanked her. I couldn't believe it. I was going to New York City! Finally.

It wasn't like I was going to just any place. A dream was about to be fulfilled. A fantasy realized. For some reason, I knew I was going to a place where I belonged.

* * *

Five months later, as planned, we went on our vacation to New York City - Mom, me, Nana, and Bubba. To summarize, it was the best trip of my life.

Nana had wanted to go in November - to see for herself the Macy's Day parade - so we made that part of our itinerary. But that wasn't all.

I saw my first musical, *The Phantom of the Opera*. We ate at Tavern on the Green. I saw 1980s New York rats, which were the size of cats, watched Bubba turn white while riding in a cab, and chanted "Save Woody" with a group of people watching the Macy's Day Parade as the Woody Woodpecker balloon started to deflate.

Beyond all of the excitement and splendor, I also saw the darker side of the city when, while eating in a restaurant, a homeless man wondered in. I peered up at him. He was disheveled and dirty. We me each other's gaze - there was a tremendous loneliness in his eyes.

And while he was being escorted out simply asked "to eat." It's an image that has stayed with me.

New York changed me in so many ways during that trip.

As we were leaving on the bus to go to the airport and home to Wisconsin, I looked out the window and wondered when I'd be back to this intoxicating city. All I could hear in my head was *thirty-six. You'll be back when you're thirty-six.*

I thought that number had to be wrong, but as it turned out, it wasn't.

Life happened, and I forgot all about my dream to live in New York City and write musicals for the Broadway stage. I wouldn't return to New York until I was thirty-six years old.

Chapter Two

Finding Oz

Twenty years later

I don't know how to paint the picture of how mundane my life had become after I went to New York City when I was sixteen, except to say that, when I look back on it now, it was as if I were asleep for twenty years. Most people seemed to think that the 'awakening' I needed should have come in the form of a handsome prince. As much as I fantasized about that prince coming into my life, I knew, at the time, I probably needed to work on myself first.

It wasn't that I didn't want to fall in love. I did. My life was in a good place - I was living in Appleton, Wisconsin. I had a good job working at the Fox Cities Performing Arts Center as the Education Coordinator. I had a nice apartment, two cats, but, for some reason, I was really unhappy.

I thought it was because I knew this was it for me. Yup, if this was going to be it for the rest of my life I knew the following things: 1) I was going to be alone forever, 2) I was going to be overweight and getting fatter, and 3) I was going to stay in that position at the performing arts center for the rest of my life.

It may be a pessimistic view—okay, it's more like a fatalistic view—but that's how I felt. Desperate, alone, and poor. Everyone's life was moving forward but mine was at a stand still.

My friend, Josie, was single, too. We worked in an office with mostly women, and in Wisconsin where people are disgustingly nice (I mean that in the nicest possible way), we held a party for every occasion known to women. There wasn't a week that went by without a birthday party, bridal shower, baby shower, or other type of celebration—which may sound fabulous, but when you have nothing happening in your life, it's a constant reminder.

Josie was my lifeline. We would plaster smiles on our faces during the parties, waiting for that big piece of cake to fill the void in our lives. It never happened.

We admitted our unhappiness to each other while watching reruns of *The Office* at one of our apartments, dosing ourselves with cheesy snacks and chocolate. We laughed about our situation mostly. For me, there was something else missing too.

Josie was obsessed with the musical, *Rent*. Her obsession can be compared to my own obsession with New York City. She had seen the musical several times in different cities. She had all the swag, and when I'd mention Adam Pascal, the actor who originated the role of Rodger, she would nearly go into orgasmic convulsions. She shared all things *Rent* with me, too.

I purchased tickets to see the show when it first went on tour. It came to Green Bay, but I was moving at the time. Sadly, I lost the tickets. I found them years later which made me laugh. When I finally did see the show, it was with Josie, and her love of the show made me love it even more.

The first time we saw it together was in Chicago. We took the train down from Milwaukee with two girlfriends from work. The entire train ride to Chicago, we imagined how

   Dorothy Never Got Down Like This

fabulous it would be if the show would come to the PAC (where we worked). It did a year later. The best part was, some of the original cast members would be performing.

I didn't think Josie would survive the announcement or the time in between, but somehow she managed, and all the sweeter, she met Adam Pascal.

During Josie's *Rent* obsession, she told me about the writer, Jonathan Larson. I knew he had written it, but I knew very little about the man. Josie loaned me a book about his life, which included his process of writing the musical. I was pursuing a career as a playwright and was very interested in other writers' stories.

As I read the first page, I learned about the night before *Rent* premiered on Broadway. Jonathan Larson died of an aortic dissection believed to have been caused by Marfan syndrome which hadn't been diagnosed in him prior to his passing.

I screamed. Then I pulled myself together and called Josie.

"*What?* How did I not know this?" I asked her.

"I don't know," Josie said.

The man had done so many amazing things in such a short amount of time. He wrote two Broadway musicals—*Tick, Tick, Boom* and *Rent*. He, even though he didn't know it at the time, brought the Broadway theatre world a new audience. He also tackled tough taboo topics of the time like homosexuality and AIDS.

My "something missing" in my life was coming to the surface. A mutual friend, Cade, helped remind me of my dream.

Cade and I had met in Appleton, but he was so unlike anyone I'd ever known before. He'd grown up in Iowa but had lived all over the country. He was well educated, had taught mathematics at NYU, was well traveled, had a great sense of humor and he was a writer.

We met through an event at work and agreed it would be a good idea to start a playwriting group. So, one night, Cade and I got together at a local coffee shop and brainstormed what we wanted our group to be like, what we were going to call it, and other details like finding a place to meet.

As I wrote down our ideas, my pen ran out of ink, and there it was, our name. We'd call our humble group of playwrights The Dying Pen.

We met once a week, inviting anyone in the community to join us and read what they were working on—usually it was plays or screenplays. Every few months, we produced the shows, which were mostly ten-minute plays.

Cade and I kicked off the event with each of us writing three plays from the perspective of a man and a woman: one based on sex, one based on marriage, and one based on death. We called the six short plays collaboratively *His & Hers*.

Our plan was to present the plays at the local coffee café and advertise our group, hopefully to gain a few more members. We gave ourselves a few weeks to write the plays. Through the process, I noticed I suddenly felt as if I was waking up. I was more passionate about my work as well as my writing - The Dying Pen had brought me back to life.

Cade's plays were as clever as they were humorous, with one of his shows being about spawning salmon, a metaphor for people trying to hook up. One of the main characters,

Chum, was a wannabe player. All six of the shows fit the bill, and I felt as though life was starting to make sense again.

Of course, it was then that the rug got pulled out from under me.

Cade had been working at a museum, and due to cutbacks, had been laid off. It wouldn't have been that big of a deal as he could do just about anything, but he had a wife and children to support. He wasn't in love with the area, so Cade prepared to make a move.

I, on the other hand, went full speed ahead with our shows. I had secured a venue, set up auditions, and was ready to cast actors when Cade gave me the news. He and his family were moving to Lancaster, Pennsylvania.

My heart sank.

Cade's presence made me feel alive in a way I had never felt before. I had someone to write with who understood my challenges. He had been places I hadn't and could share his worldly insights. I felt as though my world was bigger because I knew him. Now he was leaving.

It looked like it would be the death of The Dying Pen before it even started. I tried to put my feelings aside and be supportive for Cade's sake. However, a big part of me knew I was losing my best friend. Still, he encouraged me to go ahead with the plays.

I laughed at his suggestion. "Who will direct them?"

"You will, Erin," he said confidently.

Funny, I'd never thought of that. I'd assumed he would.

We left the café and sat in my car, talking for a long time that night. Cade asked what I was going to do.

I jokingly told him I'd apply to grad school in New York.

"Well, you should," he said. "You're talented."

I assured him I was joking. "What grad school in New York would take me? How would I even be able to go if they *did* take me?" I laughed.

"Really, Erin, I'm not kidding. You should do it."

That was a dream I never took seriously, but hearing those words from Cade, someone I really admired, made me stop and think about it.

Could I really apply to Graduate school in New York?

It's funny how you don't think about doing anything crazy until you have nothing else to lose. I suppose if I'd been completely fulfilled with what I was doing, I probably wouldn't have wanted to leave. It's like eating American cheese for years and then having a bit of aged cheddar. I wanted that taste of passion and satisfaction to continue.

Cade moved to Pennsylvania and I did what we planned. I went ahead with the six shows. I held auditions and met some amazing actors in the community—Tara and Mark, in particular.

Tara is this woman who is beautiful and funny—you think you want to hate her, but you can't. She's lovable down to her tiny waist and huge tits.

Mark is this dark horse who looks meek and mild but has the acting chops of Woody Allen. Brilliantly self-effacing and funny. I was thrilled they both showed up to audition. After casting was complete, we held rehearsals in one of the actor's homes. If you have ever done any community theatre you probably know it is always a struggle to find a rehearsal space. I have very fond and funny memories of all of us cramming into one of the actor's attics, sweating profusely and trying not to think about it. There was an incredible sense of camaraderie with this group that was unforgettable. I don't remember being hot or uncomfortable, I just remember laughing and never wanting the rehearsal process to end.

But it did. After a few weeks we set up shop at the Café. That space also proved to be interesting. It was a community Café and outreach of Goodwill, so often times people would be playing chess or checkers in the back of the room during one of our dress rehearsals. I remember one night during a performance a few people were playing an intensely loud dice game. I was about to quietly and politely ask them to move to the other room when an audience member turned around and did it for me.

Once we made it through dress rehearsals and timed the shows, I was pleased to see that we had a full hour of one-acts. We would have three performances held over a weekend. I didn't know who, if anyone, would show up.

Little did I know.

The shows were sold out! Not that there were a lot of seats, maybe 75 tops, but we had to add chairs. I was astonished. It seemed the gods had smiled upon us.

Our audiences were great too—laughing loudly in the right spots. Who knew? The response from the audience and the community was unexpected and astonishing. Not to mention that we had put on the plays with little to no money.

Again, I started to realize what the missing piece was in my life. It wasn't just working in the theatre. It was creating theatre, a dream I had forgotten about, much like my dream of living in New York City. Both of which still seemed impossible.

The plays closed, and I slipped back into that depression that one slips into after something you love goes away. It was a struggle to stay upbeat.

On the plus side, I had gained two new members for The Dying Pen. We had weekly meetings working to continue to hone our craft. I knew it would be another six months before we'd be able to perform new shows. The adrenalin had waned again, or so I thought.

One day, as I was sitting in my cubicle at work, I received an email from Susan Rabideau. She had seen our plays and wanted to produce them at the University of Wisconsin-Fox Valley, a two-year technical college in Appleton.

I was floored! Another unexpected and astonishing outcome. The sudden surge in elation was exactly what I needed at that moment.

I emailed Cade to tell him the news. He couldn't believe it, either. Even the vice president of the PAC congratulated me on our success with my small playwriting group. I had a hard time believing it was real, but it was.

There was a small hiccup in all the happiness, however. Or perhaps it wasn't a hiccup but rather a shove forward in the right direction.

I'd finally met my proverbial prince in the form of a

short, witty socialist named Garret. I really don't want to give Garret any more credit than he's due, but in hind sight, had I not met him, I may not have done the crazy things I did.

I met Garret during the run of the *His & Hers* shows. He happened to be my sound guy. Well, actually, he was a barista/bartender/sound guy. Employees at the café wore many hats.

He had thick glasses like Buddy Holly had used, wore a fedora—never a bad look for a guy—and was three inches shorter than me. What he lacked in height he made up with his dry sense of humor.

I wasn't sure if Garret filled the void that Cade had left, but there was a sincere quality about him that I hadn't experienced with a man before. He was a minimalist, content with the little things in life—something I needed to take a lesson from, what with my obsessions on how little I had or *thought* I had.

He kept me laughing through the entire production process, and somehow, we found ourselves out one night with the cast at the local gay bar watching a drag show. It was my thirty-sixth birthday and I had told Garret I'd always wanted to kiss a drag queen. Why they would want to kiss a chubby, white girl back, I don't know, but enough dollar bills can buy anything in a club.

Garret pushed me forward into a fabulously dressed queen and I got my kiss. It was lipstick on lipstick but sexy, nonetheless.

Josie, who'd come with us and could see what was happening, asked me how I felt afterwards. I told her it was the most fun I'd had on my birthday in a long time, and it was.

Garret and I were as united as two socialists at an Ayn

Rand rally. He would send me texts at work, and every time I'd hear the chirp of my phone, I was like Pavlov's dog, salivating for more Garret.

He came to visit me at work one day and I gave him a tour of the PAC. We did laundry together—we could have a fun time doing anything.

Then suddenly it stopped.

What we had ended abruptly with no explanation. He had gone somewhere to see someone and met two women who I imagined were like two sirens in the night, calling to him and pulling him from his car to have sex with them.

To be fair, I don't know if that's what happened. He stopped texting me one afternoon and I never had an answer why. Of course, I blamed myself.

Note to women out there—don't blame yourselves.

I was stunned. After years of wondering why I couldn't hold a relationship, it happened. I went a little stir crazy. I remember thinking that this was it. No more relationships. Men had hurt me for the last time.

Then, I had an epiphany. I was sitting in my big, puffy chair at home, eating cheese and sobbing when I threw down my block of cheddar, wiped my face, and stood up with my hands on my hips.

"That's it. I'm applying to grad school in New York!" I said out loud to the room.

I sat back down, picked up the cheese, and started crying.

   Dorothy Never Got Down Like This

Yea, right. You're not going anywhere.

But I was. I had to leave for survival.

Chapter Three

The Tornado
(in the form of grad school applications)

Despite the depression from Garret's abrupt leaving, I decided I was going to apply to three different graduate schools. I was thirty-six, broke, and single, so why not? What else was I doing?

I didn't think for a second any of the schools would accept me, but I had to try. Next was figuring out what to apply for? I wanted to get into a playwriting program but that didn't seem exactly right. While mulling around the idea at work, I learned that the producer of *Wicked*, David Stone, would be speaking with us before the Wisconsin premiere of the show. We were lucky enough to be the first stop on the tour, so Stone was coming to get us excited about promoting his show.

Josie and I made our way downstairs to the stage that morning. I was feeling unusually enthusiastic about the presentation, but I wasn't sure why.

When we were all seated and silenced, Stone came out and stood behind a podium in front of a large screen. He wasn't a large man, but he had a powerful presence. He spoke of how the piece began, and an image was projected on the screen of Steven Schwartz—the composer and lyricist of the musical.

Schwartz spoke, telling us how he came up with the idea for the musical, admitting he had heard about it on a scuba diving trip when a friend told him that she was reading the book of the same name.

 Dorothy Never Got Down Like This

After Schwartz finished, Stone came back onto the stage and spoke again. He invited two cast members from the West Coast touring group to come out and sing the song "For Good" from the show.

As they began to sing, I started to cry. Tears streamed uncontrollably down my face. Josie looked over at me, shocked.

"What's wrong?" she asked. "Are you okay?"

"I want to do this," I whispered, fighting back a sobbing squeak.

"Be in *Wicked*?"

"No, write musicals," I said.

But how? I'm a straight, broke, white girl living in the Midwest. Who cares about what I have to say?

I cried until Stone finished his speech. Everybody noticed, but I had no excuse. I knew I had to find a way to write musicals.

I left work that day and went to a nearby piano studio. Bruce, a man who was one of the piano teachers, asked me why I wanted to take lessons.

"Because I want to write musicals," I admitted to him.

He looked at me oddly, but then smiled. "Why don't we start by learning some scales."

I spent the next year trying to learn to play piano. I think learning an instrument when you're an adult is the equivalent of putting your head in a vice and squeezing it. I knew how to read music, but only treble clef, not bass clef or any others. It felt like I was learning a new language and it was one of the most difficult things to grasp. I had so many moments where I felt like that Muppet on Sesame Street who would pound his head on the piano keys and shout, "I'm no good, I'm no good!"

After hearing Stone speak, I knew there was only one program I wanted to explore and only one school I wanted to attend. New York University's Tisch School of the Arts. Tisch had the only program in the country for musical theatre writing. That was it—the pinnacle, the beacon, the hot, oozing cheddar cheese on top of the nacho. It was exclusive, expensive, and there was no possible way I'd ever get accepted.

With the odds against me, I made my decision to apply to Tisch. I also decided to apply to two playwriting programs in New York; Brooklyn College (which seemed lovely and affordable) and Sarah Lawrence. Lawrence sounded classy and they were still accepting applications. Once I made my choices, I read over the application process and gathered everything I needed.

Little did I know that completing the applications was kind of like plucking out all of my body hairs one-by-one; it's long, painful, and it hurts when you're finished.

After completing the applications, I sent them to my prospective universities and waited.

I've never been a patient person—it's not my strong suit, so I was checking the mailbox and my email a minute after I hit send. I had to remind myself that it was going to take a while for any replies.

Or not.

The first letter I received was from Sarah Lawrence

Dorothy Never Got Down Like This

University. It came so quickly I wondered if they'd even read my application. It was in a rather thin envelope with red writing in the corner. I knew what it was going to say before I opened it.

Sure enough, the first line started with *We are sorry to inform you—*

It was like dealing with a death. Why do they have to start letters like that? Why can't they start them with something like *You're fabulous! Thanks for applying you fabulous person you! You're too good for us, which is why we can't accept you."*

Even if it's a lie, it would soften the blow.

One down, and I had only applied to three schools.

After receiving that letter from Sarah Lawrence, I thought I was never going to get out of Wisconsin. I'd die alone in my apartment on my couch with a half-eaten block of cheese resting on my chest and a dirty scene from some TV series stuck in pause on the television screen.

I resigned myself to remain numb. I'd go to work, taking all of these fabulous actors to workshops and envying their conversations about life in New York. I felt my eyes glaze over every time they'd talk about it. It was too painful to think that my last shot at my dream was fading along with my waistline. I didn't care anymore. I couldn't. What was the point?

It was an unseasonably warm day in March when I got a call from an unfamiliar number. I heard my cell phone vibrate in my purse as I was sitting in my cubicle. I reached in and grabbed it. The first three numbers were 212.

Oh snap, the 212 is calling for me. I'm a dork. Of course,

I knew one of the area codes for New York is 212.

I couldn't contain my enthusiasm. I ran down to one of the dressing rooms in the theatre, knowing they were empty and quickly answered the call.

"Hello, Erin?"

"Yes," I said.

"This is Jeanette Esquela calling from Tisch School of the Arts. I'm calling to let you know that you haven't completed the application. Did you want to finish it?"

I couldn't speak. I uttered an "Ah, yeah." *What didn't I finish?*

"Okay, great. I'll email you the link. Fill it out and email it back to us by Monday. Okay?"

"Ah-huh," I mumbled.

"Thank you."

I hit END on my phone to disconnect the call and stood there staring at *The Lion King* poster on the wall in front of me. *Tisch called me.*

"Tisch called me!" I screamed at the poster.

I darted upstairs to find Josie. I grabbed her out of her chair and yanked her into the hallway. "You're never going to believe what just happened. You're never going to believe it." My smile was so big I felt like I had an instant facelift.

"What, what is it?" she asked.

"Tisch just called me. *Tisch!*"

We screamed and jumped up and down like two giddy contestants on *The Price Is Right*. We couldn't believe it. *I* couldn't believe it. The phone call was so surreal. Now I had to finish the application.

No problem.

When I opened the link Jeanette had sent me, I wanted to swallow my own tongue. What I had failed to fill out was pages and pages of essay questions, many of which called for samples of lyrics.

I had found it strange that they didn't ask for writing samples in the portion of the application I had filled out. I didn't question it though, or even try to write lyrics during the long waiting period. Now, I had until Monday to write some, and it was Friday.

I scribbled down some words and went to see Bruce to get his opinion.

He read over my first attempt at a lyric, then crinkled his face. Had he just sucked on a lemon?

"This doesn't sound like a lyric, Erin. It sounds like a grocery list."

Eek, okay. I gave him my second attempt, but his face puckered up again.

"A lyric should be singable. This sounds like a random stream of consciousness."

Which, in all honesty it was. I had no clue what I was doing. No clue, and the deadline was fast approaching. How had I gotten a call from Tisch?

Then I remembered Cade's words. He had reminded me that I was worthy of attending Tisch, noting the success of The Dying Pen.

Maybe I was worthy, but I still had no clue how to complete the application. I tried to tell myself that I wouldn't get accepted. After all, it was highly unlikely that I would. I tried to relax, forget about the deadline, and write some coherent lyrics.

I realized quickly that lyric writing for the theatre is not just jotting down sentences that rhyme. It's writing in a character's voice along with a conversational tone, matching the scansion from verse to verse, making sure it's the right dramatic moment—all of which aren't easy things to do.

I had no time to practice, so I stayed up all night and finally produced something worth showing to Bruce, or at least I hoped so. I had written two songs, one that I thought was decent and one that I hated, but I needed two.

On Saturday morning, I rushed over to see Bruce. He was in the middle of teaching lessons. I waited until he finished before I peeked into his studio.

"I've got something," I said, holding the paper out for him to read.

Bruce appeared underwhelmed at first, but when he read the lyrics his face lit up. "When did you write this?" he asked.

"Last night. I haven't slept," I said, rubbing my eyes.

"If you can write this under pressure than don't go to sleep, write more. It's good. Hurry up!"

I wanted to hug Bruce. I had some decent lyrics to send,

thank God. Now for the rest of the application.

Luckily, I received another call from the 212. It was Jeanette Esquela letting me know that the school was going on spring break. I wouldn't have to return the application until the following Monday.

It was an amazing stroke of luck. I had a week to complete it, and thank heavens for that, because I wrote more lyrics and had more time to perfect my thoughts. I sent it off a week later and breathed a sigh of relief. I had finished the application.

As I waited for a response, I started to doubt myself. Was what I sent good enough? Am *I* good enough? Who am I to think I have any right to go to Tisch? The negative stream of thoughts filled my head. Not to mention, I received a rejection letter from Brooklyn College. It was a ridiculously short email. Gee, thanks.

Things weren't looking good.

I went to bed that night sure I would hear a big NO from Tisch. I went to sleep wondering if I should've even bothered.

That night I dreamt.

There was a stove at the edge of my bed, up against the wall near the window. And there he stood—Jonathan Larson, creator of the musical Rent, *cooking me breakfast. He was making scrambled eggs.*

He looked at me with a wide, beaming smile as if he'd known me forever.

I laid there for a moment staring at him, not sure what

to make of the situation. Then I said, "I have no business going to Tisch."

He flipped the eggs onto a plate, handed it to me, and said ever so kindly, "Of course you do."

I took a bite of the eggs and smiled back at him.

Then I woke up.

I laughed out loud and spoke to the empty room. "Well, if Jonathan Larson says I can go, then I'll go—if I get in, that is."

A few days later, I got the call from the 212. It was Jeanette Esquela asking if I'd talked to the financial aid office.

I was confused.

She must have noticed my lack of response because she asked, "You do know you've been accepted, Erin?"

Chapter Four

Click Your Heels Together Three Times.
Each One Will Cost Ya' a Thousand Dollars

I'm not sure how Dorothy felt when she stepped out of her house into Oz, but when it sank in that I'd be moving to New York to attend grad school at New York University in less than six months, I wished for a good witch to pop out of her bubble and show me the way.

Let me revisit childhood for a moment. I come from a tiny peninsula in Wisconsin. My family is made up of fishermen. They've lived on boats, gutted fish, ate Herring, drank beer, chopped wood, and when not on boats, they hide in cabins in the woods. These are not city people. To be someone who wants to live in a large city coming from this clan, well, it becomes a bit of a puzzlement in the mind of someone like, say, my father. He still can't figure out what it is I love about New York.

Yes, even for me, someone who spent her entire life yearning to go to New York City, it was going to be a bit of an adjustment. Remember, the biggest city I'd lived in thus far was Green Bay with roughly 100,000 people. It was where I had attended undergrad, but as nice as Green Bay is, it had never felt like home.

The first thing I had to do was send my deposit to NYU. I looked at Josie after I wrote the check.

"I'm securing my spot," I said, unable to accept it was real.

How was this my new reality? A part of me couldn't believe it. I still thought the rug was going to be pulled out from underneath me any minute.

At the previous year's Thanksgiving holiday after I'd applied, Dad made some mention of it to the extended family—that I was thinking of attending grad school in New York. The room fell silent. Nobody said anything.

And then everyone went back to the turkey and stuffing their faces.

I glanced around the room and felt disappointment due to the lack of my family's reaction. Maybe to them it was one more thing that wouldn't come to fruition for me. After all, there'd been failed attempts at a lot of things—jobs, romances, even an engagement I'd called off at age twenty-five. My family knew when to approach with caution.

The truth is, when someone we love plans to move, the silence is really the stillness of hope. People don't like change. My family was no exception. They didn't want to see me go to a strange, big city alone.

I'm picturing myself as Little Red Riding Hood carrying a basket of cannoli pastries to my neighbor's house in Astoria, fighting off wolves in the shape of swarthy Greek men. How bad would that be? (Spoiler alert: sexy chapter ahead.)

My family was right to be worried, because I was worried.

I couldn't just send a deposit and think it was all going to work out. I had to find an apartment, have money to pay for it, have money to pay for school, food, the list went on… Money was the main thing I needed. Lots and lots of *money!*

The only way I was going to get to my Oz (NYC) was to come up with a lot of green. My world wouldn't be changing anytime soon unless I came up with a lot of money—but how?

I equate moving to New York to vacationing in Las Vegas, but not as easy. You arrive and you're ecstatic! Everything's shiny and new. The lights are flashing in your face, disorienting you. You want to go everywhere and see everything, so you do. The next thing you know, you've lost all of your money at Blackjack. You check your wallet and there's nothing left. You hit the ATM and that's empty, too.

What did I buy besides a burger, fries, and tickets to Avenue Q?

That's New York in a nutshell. Everything costs something. If it doesn't cost something, there's something wrong.

I learned quickly not to get excited about things like, say, an empty subway car, because when the doors opened there was the stench of bodily fluids somebody had left behind. Or, when I was running around Times Square and had to use the bathroom, but first I needed to buy dinner for $67.50 to use the rest room.

Coming from Wisconsin, I was completely naïve and way too nice for my own good. I was an easy target. I had no idea how much moving and then attending NYU was going to cost me.

Beyond the expense, I was terrified. I had no idea how I'd do any of it.

There are people (like Garret) who tout the idea of selling all of your worldly possessions to experience a sense of peace and harmony to be one with the universe. *Yea, because you're sleeping on it.*

I had done the Midwestern thing and had a garage sale at my friend Polly's house. Polly is a fabulous friend who not only has given me numerous rides to and from the airport, she was kind enough to let me use her garage to sell my stuff. She didn't live that far from me, and since my apartment wasn't conducive for a garage sale, we had it at Polly's.

When I sold all of my stuff, I had no idea how hard it would be to watch everything I owned walk down the street with a stranger. It was then that I realized I had nothing left—literally—nothing left but the clothes in my suitcase. I don't know if I would call that a cleanse or an enema. I thought I no longer had any attachment to my things, but as I saw people picking through my Christmas decorations and old trunks, I remembered how much I'd liked that apartment in Appleton, not to mention having the best group of friends I'd ever had in my lifetime—including Polly and Josie.

I had my eye on the prize for so long that I hadn't taken a second to look at what I was giving up. Besides my close friends, I was leaving a community that embraced me as a writer, a playwriting group that I'd established, not to mention my family, with nieces and nephews who I loved like they were my own kids.

It was all starting to sink in my thick skull that I was moving far away, and I still had no clue how I was paying to live in New York. Or how to get there.

After we packed up the last items that hadn't sold, Polly handed me $200, which I was thrilled to get, but I was tempted to take it to the casino. *Maybe if I put it all on red or black?* I knew it was only the beginning of what I'd need.

Still, I'm a big believer that God provides. I knew it was

going to work out.

I called my new best friend, Jeanette Esquela, to ask her for advice. She said several people had held concerts to earn money to come to Tisch, and then she joked, "Or you can go into copious amounts of debt."

I received my financial aid letter in the mail and my jaw dropped. While it was enough to get me to New York and pay for school, I wasn't sure if I would ever be able to pay it back, even if I sold every organ I could part with, and then some.

But when you're chasing a dream, money doesn't seem to matter.

To recap what to do when chasing a dream.

After getting accepted—much to your surprise—into your perfect degree program, sell everything you own, realize everything you own is worth a very measly amount, and brainstorm ways to make money. (Don't follow through on the illegal items on your list. Well, maybe not *all* of the illegal items on your list.)

I had enough financial aid to pay for grad school. I still had to figure out rent—there's a reason the musical *Rent* is set in New York.

The selling continued.

I sold my bike—a black and green Trek I'd had since I was fourteen. (Man, did I love that bike!) I sold my car and used my grandmother's because she was no longer driving. I didn't think I had it in me to sell everything that I owned, but when I saw the last of my Buddha candle collection make its way down the street in the hands of some happy person who visited my garage sale, it was solidified.

While moving my bed down into the basement of my parents' house I had a startling thought. *Dear God, what have I done?*

Suddenly, it was a reality.

Chapter Five

Unhitched and Unhinged

There's a great lyric from *The Wizard of Oz* by the incredibly talented Yip Harburg about hinges getting unhitched. That's how I felt trying to prepare for the biggest transition of my life - unhitched and unhinged.

Once I knew I was accepted to NYU, things moved quickly. The closer it got to August, the more I started to panic. There was so much to do. I knew if I stopped to think about it, I would talk myself out of the incredible opportunity ahead of me. I was determined not to let fear paralyze me.

I worked with a lot of fabulous people at the PAC in Appleton. Two of them, Terrie and Joe, owned a travel agency. When they heard the news, they invited me to go along with them to New York in May.

I wanted to take a tour of NYU and get an idea of where to look for housing. I knew nothing about New York, except that I wanted to live there since birth. (You'd think I would've checked out a map of the city or something.)

Everything was arranged with Terrie and Joe, and we were set to go. I was so thrilled to make my first trip back at the age of thirty-six.

They picked me up early on the day of the trip. I slept in the back of their car on the way to General Mitchell Airport in Milwaukee. Once we were seated on the plane awaiting take off, I was so excited I felt like I could fly to the Big Apple on my own. The excitement soon turned into nerves, as the saliva evaporated from my mouth as if I just drank a bottle of Chardonnay and ate a block of salty cheese - never a bad thing, except when you haven't done either of those things!

I wasn't a great flyer. I'm much better at it now, but back then, I'd flown only a handful of times. The thought of leaving the ground made me sweat. The first time I flew was my trip to New York when I was sixteen. Again, I was so excited, I begged Mom to let me sit near the window. I gazed out, seeing everything during takeoff. When the plane began to turn on its side, my stomach did the same thing, and needless to say, I was really grateful for the bag that ever so conveniently had been placed in the back of the seat in front of me. Mom had to chuckle, having predicted what was going to happen, but of course, I didn't listen.

Luckily, the flight with Terrie and Joe wasn't as bad. Terrie was kind enough to bump us up closer to the front of the plane to business class, telling me, "It'll make flying easier."

And it did. I was comfortable, and once we were in the air, I wasn't anxious. The pieces of the puzzle were all coming together.

When the plane touched down, Terrie pointed out the window at the Welcome to New York sign with the big apple in the middle.

I felt a smile stretch across my face that could only be prompted by seeing New York City.

In the cab, on the way to the hotel, my eyes were darting around at everything. I couldn't take in the sights fast enough.

Terrie leaned over to me and said, "Erin, this is where

you're going to live."

My eyes welled up with tears. She was right. This was where I was going to live. My dream was coming to fruition. I couldn't believe it!

"You'll have to find a rich guy," she said, joking.

Without batting an eyelash, I said, "I'll make my own money." And somehow, I knew I would be able to take care of myself while I was there.

We arrived at the hotel in the center of Times Square. As we got out of the cab, I stood, total tourist, eyes-wide, taking in everything. The steam coming from the street, the scads of people milling about, and, my favorite thing - the abundance of Broadway billboards that flashed names of my favorite titles at me. I shut my eyes and hoped that one day my musical would take up one of the marquees in the Broadway district. *It will happen, Erin.* I had to believe it myself.

We dropped off our bags at the hotel, but we were too early to check-in. To kill time, we went to see *La Cage Aux Folles* on Broadway, starring Kelsey Grammar.

We sat in the last row against the wall near the door. We had purchased the last three remaining seats before curtain.

The performances were excellent, but during the show I could hear police sirens. I was so tired yet so awake, all I could ask myself was, *Is this really where I'm going to live for two years?*

After the show, we headed to the hotel and crashed. We were exhausted.

Then we freshened up and headed out into the craziness

of Times Square that evening. We ate dinner at a restaurant called The Pig and Whistle on a balcony overlooking a side street in Times Square. For a moment, I felt as if I were in a movie. The bright lights, various smells, and array of unfamiliar sounds were a constant stream of stimulation.

Terrie must have noticed the expression on my face because she looked at Joe. She laughed and said, "Look at her."

Joe did and smiled. "She's overwhelmed."

Boy, was I.

After dinner, Terrie wanted to go dancing and I concurred. There was nothing more - absolutely nothing - that I liked better than dancing. I wanted to dance until dawn!

We walked around the blocks surrounding the hotel - we didn't want to go too far away - and ended up at The Pig and Whistle again, which had dancing. It was overcrowded and sweltering. I was sweating within minutes of getting on the dance floor and I loved every minute of it!

We met two gentlemen from India. We danced with them until 2:30 AM, closing down the bar.

Completely drunk and physically exhausted, I stumbled out of the place, leaning on Joe's shoulder. He and Terrie laughed at my low tolerance and refused to take me back to the hotel until we'd properly wandered around Times Square.

Apparently, that meant getting a foot-long hot dog from one of the local street vendors. With me at one end and Terrie at the other, we nibbled on the hot dog while Joe took a photo of us. Something we had totally forgotten about doing until we saw it the next day.

Eventually, we made our way to the hotel. In my inebriated state, I flopped onto the bed and laid there fully clothed. My thoughts were reeling.

I called my younger brother. Mind you, it was probably 4 AM.

"Tim. Hi. It's your sister, Erin. How are you?" Apparently, I was feeling chatty.

"It's early," he said, with a sort of question in his voice.

"Yes, but how am I going to do this?" I asked him.

He laughed. Asked if I was drunk, and then said, "You can do it. I know you can. You can do anything."

Sure, I could. Why not?

He believed in me and I wanted to believe him. I apologized for calling while I was drunk and in the middle of the night. Then I said good-bye and went to sleep.

It was 7 AM when the alarm blasted into the room like a subway car with bad brakes. *Who had set the alarm anyway?*

Oh. It was me, because I had a tour scheduled at NYU at nine o'clock.

I sat up and slammed my hand on the snooze button. I looked around the room to see which one of them I would have to wake up to go with me. Terrie had one arm hanging off the edge of the bed and a pillow half over her head. Joe was still in his clothes from the night before. He had fallen asleep in the chair in the corner of the room while undoing his shirt. His head was resting akimbo on the back of the chair and he was snoring.

The alarm went off again.

Joe's head bounced forward as if he were a bobble head doll. He wiped a stream of drool from his chin. "Huh, what?"

"I hate to do this to you, but I have to go to NYU for that tour this morning."

Joe glanced at Terrie, who mumbled something inaudible. I think it was "foot long hot dog."

He sat up, rubbed his eyes, and said he'd go with me, which was kind of him since he was running on less than four hours of sleep.

We got ready quickly and made our way to the lobby. A gentleman working there, who I will never forget, asked me where I was headed. I told him the cross streets. He told us to follow him outside. He leaned into the car of a waiting cab, and told the driver, "Take this lovely young lady to NYU."

Wow. That made me feel like royalty.

We slid into the cab, and Joe tried to catch a few z's leaning against the side of the door while we flew down the street. I enjoyed the energy of the zinging taxi as my heart hummed along with the movement of the city. My thoughts were positive and happy that morning.

I think I'm gonna like it here.

* * *

At NYU, I had the strangest sense of déjà vu as I stepped out onto the curb. I knew I hadn't been there before, so I took it as a good sign.

We made our way into the Visitor's Center and awaited the start of our tour.

To begin, we listened to a speaker for an hour. While I was hanging on her every word, soaking up as much as I could about NYU, Joe fought to stay awake. I was glad we sat in the back of the room so he could rest his head on the wall. I think I would've had more of a hangover, too, had I not been so excited.

The speaker covered the cost of four years of undergraduate school at NYU and I saw a few parents around me swallow hard. I didn't know how I was going to pay for two years of grad school, I couldn't imagine having to figure out how to swing four years.

At the end of the session, the speaker asked each of us to stand up and introduce ourselves. She pointed at me and asked me to start. She told me to say my name, age, and if I was planning to attend. If yes, what I wanted to major in.

I stood up, felt everyone's eyes on me, smiled brightly, and said, "My name is Erin Hunsader. I've been accepted into the Graduate Musical Theatre Writing Program at Tisch School of the Arts."

I heard a kid say "wow" quietly to himself in support of me.

I went on. "I live in Wisconsin, and this was the only time I could take a tour before starting this fall."

I sat back down as the speaker said, "Congratulations. Welcome to NYU."

I met her gaze and felt my eyes well up with tears. My dream was finally coming true. By autumn, I'd be living in

New York and attending NYU.

Or was I? I still had no place to live, no idea how I was moving there and no money. Just a few minor details that I needed to figure out - and fast. August was right around the corner.

Chapter Six

Landing in Oz

Funny how when one part of your life starts to become fabulous other parts tend to turn into big dung heaps.

On the return home from New York, I phoned my family from the airport to tell them about the trip.

When I called my brother, Tim, my seven-year-old nephew, Gabriel, answered the phone. Without even saying hello, he said, "Auntie, are you still in New York?"

He had apparently talked to Tim.

"No," I said, "I'm on my way home now."

"What were you doing there?" he asked in his little voice.

"I went there to take a tour of New York University."

"Why?"

"Well, I've been accepted to go to school there. I'm going to pursue my master's degree."

There was a long pause and I thought for a moment we had been disconnected.

"Are you going there?" he asked.

"Yes," I said.

"You big turd," he blurted. And he hung up.

I totally understood why he had said that. He and I were best buds, and he wasn't thrilled with this information.

My other nephew and nieces had similar reactions. I had tried to be a cool auntie, and it made me feel fabulous that they didn't want me to go. It also broke my heart.

That wasn't the worst of it. Grandpa's health was deteriorating rapidly. There's something about grandparents - they seem sort of immortal. When it looks like they're about to pass on, it seems surreal, as if they're supposed to live forever.

I was still working at the Performing Arts Center when I got a call from my parents. I heard Dad's voice on the other end and immediately knew something was wrong. *Who died?* He never called me, it was always Mom.

He told me that Bubba had taken a turn for the worst and it probably wouldn't be long.

It wasn't.

Bubba passed away that evening. I was glad he was no longer in pain. He had always said that he wanted to go fast and never end up as a burden to anyone. Still, I was grief-stricken. He had always helped me to see the good in myself.

Bubba had a fabulous sense of humor, right up until the end. He'd been diagnosed with having dementia and it took over quickly.

I remember one day in church when there was a visiting priest, who'd been playing a rather dull video focused on fund-raising. After it finished, the church was completely silent. Grandfather so eloquently summed up what everyone was thinking as he said, "Hallelujah. That's over."

I tried holding back my laughter when a few people giggled. That was Grandpa. He knew when to be serious and when to be funny, even with dementia.

Grandpa passed, and the world felt empty without him. It was very weird for me for a while. I'd been blessed to have most of my relatives around for the majority of my life.

Dad's father had passed away when I was eight, so I didn't remember much about him. He was a fisherman and loved the water. I wish I would've known him better, but fate hadn't allowed much time with him.

So, when Bubba passed, the man who was like a second father to me, I felt a deep void. I prayed a lot for him. He often contemplated over whether or not he'd make it to Heaven. I was sure he did.

Grandpa's death made me reflect on things in a different way. It put things in perspective for me. I had always thought of him as an incredibly successful person. I wondered if leaving my job at the PAC with benefits in a field I loved was the right thing to do. I was putting myself in massive amounts of debt, taking a huge risk saying yes to this graduate school program, and I wasn't even sure if I'd be able to finish it. Would he be proud of me for taking these steps to reach my full potential? Would I be proud of myself?

I had to give notice at my job. I gave myself a date of July 15th to let them know. I had to find an apartment, as dorms weren't a possibility for grad students in this particular field. Then, once I found the apartment, I'd have to figure out how I was going to pay rent. I had $1500 saved, but that'd be gone in a breath in New York.

July 15th approached. I kept playing my words over and

over in my head, wondering how it'd go down after I gave my notice. We all have our issues with jobs we've had, but with the job at the Performing Arts Center, I have to say I was blessed. The training I got there was exceptional - something I'm still grateful for.

On July 15th, I told Josie first. She knew I was leaving, of course, but I hadn't told anyone else at work. I walked into my boss' office and took a deep breath.

"Can I talk to you for a second?" I asked.

My boss, who I had come to like as a friend, looked up from what she was doing.

"Of course. What do you need?"

"I have something to tell you. This really isn't easy because I love what I do here, but I did something crazy and applied for grad school in New York, and I got in." I said it all in one breath before I lost my nerve.

My boss stared at me for a moment, probably trying to process this information, but then, without missing a bit, she was incredibly supportive.

"Well, that's amazing, Erin."

I breathed a sigh of relief. I went on to share the rest of the story with her. Then I gave my two weeks-notice.

As I stepped out of her office, I saw everything I passed on a daily basis in a different way. I saw the gray partitions of the cubicles, the aging posters on the wall of past shows, the coffee pot which made horrible coffee, and I knew I was going to miss all of it.

My boss had surprised me, being supportive in a very sincere way. As was everyone at the PAC - it's a place where everyone cheered on everyone else's successes. Might explain all the cake parties. But even with all the celebrations we held each month, I felt lucky to have had the three years of experience there.

Now the real work was about to begin.

It was nearing the end of July and I would be starting at NYU the last weekend in August. I was freaking out that I didn't have a place to live.

I decided I needed to go to New York on my own to find a place to live. (SCARY!) I called my friend, Tara, the actress I met during the Dying Pen shows. She had moved out to New York with her husband a few months earlier.

I asked Tara how she found her apartment. She recommended a real estate agency she had used.

I booked a flight and made an appointment with someone named Jerusalem at the agency. I reserved a hotel room for two nights - which was painfully expensive, but at least I had it lined up.

My family and friends threw me a party the night before I was supposed to leave. We went to the piano bar where Bruce played. I had a few too many glasses of wine, shots, and even some ice cream drinks.

Dad was concerned as he looked at me and said, "Remember, you have to get on a plane tomorrow."

It was so much fun - too much fun, actually. I felt myself not wanting to go.

I woke up late but didn't feel rushed. I stopped at the store, and still thought I'd make it to the General Mitchell airport on time. I drove to Milwaukee, not knowing how much road construction there was, and when I realized I was lost, I called Joe. (This trip happened before it was common for everyone to have GPS in their vehicles and on their phones.)

Joe wasn't much help in terms of directions, but he did say I could call the airport, let them know what happened, and see if they could get me on another flight.

Again, luck was with me.

The airline booked me into a hotel room and got me on an early flight the next day. They were accommodating, but I had to reschedule with the real estate agent. The hotel in New York charged me for the night I missed even though I gave them a full day's notice - the first time I'd lost money in New York, but not the last.

That night, I lay on my bed in the hotel room in Milwaukee, frozen with fear. I couldn't figure out why? This was my dream I was chasing. Why was I so afraid? The thought of landing in New York alone scared me to death. I closed my eyes and imagined melting into the sheets, wondering just how I thought I was going to do this back when I had applied. I forced myself to focus on my breathing and reminded myself that I had to take this next step to move forward toward my dream.

The next morning, I got up extra early. I took the shuttle to the airport and my fears seemed to have subsided.

All went well. The plane landed safely and as I stepped out of the airport, I realized that now I was a New Yorker. Then, someone shoved me from behind, knocking me out of my self-confident bubble.

Cabs whizzed by and I searched for the sign that said 'shuttles'. I had scheduled a shuttle to take me to the hotel.

The shuttle was a big, clunky van, packed with as many people as possible. We must have looked like clowns in a Volkswagen Beetle. It was 90 degrees and there was no air conditioning. So, we all sat quietly - hot, sweaty, and smelly while awaiting our drop off point. It took two hours to get to my hotel.

I was excited about where I was staying...until I saw my room. I think they had converted the janitors' closet into a guest room. The bathroom was tiny, like a bathroom on a train would be and the ceiling dipped so low I had to duck down to use the shower. I wasn't planning to look at apartments until the next day, so I stared out the barred windows, searching for something to do.

Get your butt out there and see a show.

I was staying on 28th Street, not far from the theatre district and walked to see the musical, Next to Normal. The show, which is about a woman dealing with mental illness, opened my eyes to how a musical can act as a tool to explore more serious subject matter. I wanted to write a musical that used humor, but also allowed the audience to have a depth of feeling - something different than musicals of the past that had been labeled as *fluffy*.

When the curtain closed, I stepped out of the theatre, breathed in the intoxicating New York air, and strolled down the street. As I walked to the hotel, it got foggy and the streets became unusually quiet. I felt uneasy and said a quick prayer that I was safe. I walked quickly, putting on my new assertive New York face and made it back to the hotel without incidence. I went to sleep that night with a sense of confidence I never knew I had before. I felt I could take on the world, then a ceiling tile fell on my… Ah, the joys of New York.

Chapter Seven

Someone Please Drop a House on Me
(for really cheap rent)

Never mind that I had never seen a cockroach before and the thought of when I might caused me to shutter. Minus the eminent threat of prehistoric bugs, I knew I had to find a place to live.

The next morning, I woke up and took a cab to the real estate office. The cab driver asked me the cross streets - I had no idea I needed to know that - I couldn't have been more green.

He asked me which side of the street the building was on. I didn't know that, either. I should've had a sign on my head that said, Hello, I'm from Wisconsin and I have NO CLUE!

He dropped me off in front of the building and I went in. Then, it was a matter of finding the correct floor. How I got anywhere in New York City those first few days by myself was a miracle!

I got off the elevator and saw a sea of cubicles in a large spacious room. It looked a little like a real estate sweatshop. The receptionist glanced at me as if I had the plague. I wore heavy wool shorts and a rayon shirt - not the best for the 90-degree heat and humidity. I still hadn't shed my Wisconsin fashion and I was sweating profusely.

I told her I had an appointment with Jerusalem. I had a

feeling I'd like him.

Then I heard a choir somewhere inside my imagination, as I saw a man rise from one of the cubicles - he was a tall and charismatic with coffee-colored eyes and a wide beaming smile, probably in his mid-twenties. He came over to me, shook my hand.

I held on to his for a bit too long. If the men in New York looked like Jerusalem, I never wanted to leave.

"Erin," he said, breaking me from my trance, "in missing your flight, you lost out on getting a shot at the latest listings."

I didn't think it was a big deal. I was wrong.

I discovered that as soon as apartments were put on the market in New York City, they were gone.

The first thing Jerusalem did was sit me down with Bob, a bald man with a face like a bull dog. He had squinty, piercing eyes, and a thick New York accent that made him sound as if he was yelling whenever he spoke. While I thought Bob was probably a sweetheart, he scared the shit out of me.

He didn't waste any time making small talk like Midwesterners like to do. He jumped right in and asked me about my budget, what could I spend per month on rent. My magic number in my head was $800. When I said that, Bob laughed out loud. I don't mean a chuckle, I mean a full-out guffaw.

"Erin, here's what you'll get for $800 a month." Bob proceeded to show me a picture on his computer of an 8 x 5 room in someone's basement. That was my first eye-opener.

I ran the numbers and thought I could spend up to $1650

a month, but that would leave me with nothing to live on.

I asked Bob how much I should expect to spend on a studio apartment.

Instead of answering, he asked me where I wanted to live.

I told him I needed to be near NYU.

Again, he chortled. "That's not going to happen for $800 a month. In fact, that's not going to happen at all."

"Why?" I asked, wondering if he was just messing with the clueless girl from Wisconsin.

"There's nothing available there. *Nothing!* Everybody wants to live down there."

I put my fingers to my forehead and tried to rub away the wrinkle I was making with my furrowed brow.

"Why don't we expand our search?" Bob huffed, as if he was from *The Godfather* finding me an offer I couldn't refuse.

He wound up locating some studios that had just opened up on the Upper East side. I didn't know it at the time, but that area was known as the stuffy, rich part of town. Bob assured me it was safe, which was really my only criteria.

"Tha maya lives there. Ya' can't do much betta than dat," Bob snorted.

"Well, if the mayor lives there, then it must be safe."

When I asked him how much the rent would be, he told me between $1300 - $1500.

I swallowed hard. This was my reality.

So, after crying a little on the inside while sitting across from Bob, I realized I had to give in if this dream was happening. Next, Jerusalem and I were off to look at overpriced, roach-infested spaces.

We headed to the subway.

I hadn't ridden the subway since I was sixteen. That time, I'd been with my family and a tour guide. Jerusalem told me to buy a metro card. I had thought you put change into a box (like when you get on the bus) to get on the subway - another moment of not having a clue. Jerusalem had an unlimited card, so he swiped me through.

While we were on the train, I looked for any kind of information to tell me where and when to get off. I heard a muffled, scratchy voice that sounded like Charlie Brown's teacher.

We weren't on a train with a digital sign in the middle of the car, so when Jerusalem stood up and said it was time to get off, I asked, "How did you know it was the right stop?"

He said he just knew the stops, but I was so confused.

And frustrated. *How am I going to learn all of this?*

We went to an apartment around the block of 77th and Lexington, which Jerusalem said was a great location because it was near the subway. Inside the building, it looked like a place I wouldn't want to spend a lot of time in - at least if it had been in Wisconsin, I wouldn't have.

We stepped up 5 flights of stairs before we finally reached the apartment's floor. I thought I was in pretty good shape until I felt my legs want to buckle underneath me and the first beads of sweat start down my back. I got to the top first, and Jerusalem told me the door should be open.

I turned the knob and it fell off. I was stunned.

Jerusalem started laughing as I stood there with the doorknob still in my hand. I had a feeling this was a common occurrence.

I had an idea of what the apartment would look like on the inside. Was I wrong. I thought it would be similar to a small apartment in Wisconsin - square-shaped rooms filled with lots of light from the expanse of windows lining each room. The reality was the difference between a hotel bathroom and a port-a-potty. The rooms were small, dark, and dank. But then again, this was based on my perspective coming from a place filled with wide open spaces, both inside and out, because when Jerusalem saw it, a boy born in the Bronx, he said, "Wow. This is nice!"

As I stood inside the small space, I couldn't help but think, *Where's the rest of it?*

The kitchen was about 6 feet by 2 feet, and the living space off the kitchen was around 6 feet by 6 feet. The bathroom was next to the kitchen and looked like a closet that had a toilet stuck in it. That was the entire apartment. No bedroom, no closets. I pressed the palms of my hands against my forehead as I tried to work out in my head where I would put my bed.

And then another realization hit. *Oh shit, I need a bed!*

There were cupboards in the kitchen, their integrity entirely suspect, if I ever wanted to put dishes in them or open and close the doors. There was also a brown film that covered everything - it was an extravaganza of dirt that seemed to go back to the beginning of time.

I stood there with the doorknob still in my hand, in shock.

Jerusalem glanced at me and said, "Hey, Erin, you're not going to spend a lot of time here. It's just a place to sleep."

I'm not sure I'd want to do that here.

New York apartments were so different than anywhere I'd lived in Wisconsin, and it was so much more money. I had a moment of reflection on Jack Nicholson's famous line from *A Few Good Men*, "You can't handle the truth," because in all honesty, I hadn't been prepared for this.

I asked Jerusalem to call Bob for me. Bob told us that apartment was already gone.

I wasn't sure if I should swear or do a happy dance. Little did I know that would be one of the best apartments we'd see that day.

We went to two or three more apartments in the area. One Jerusalem liked - it had a brick wall in it, a popular feature Jerusalem said people loved. The apartment was really tiny and dark, and it kind of made me feel I was in a medieval prison cell.

We continued our search.

Jerusalem showed me another one-bedroom apartment. The bedroom was big enough to put a twin-sized mattress in, and that was it. I wouldn't have even been able to walk around the bed; I'd have to stand in the doorway and fall backwards onto the bed. Even Jerusalem thought that was a bit ridiculous.

Every apartment we went to that day got smaller, dirtier,

and more expensive than the next (because even if it was a shithole, and it's a shithole near Central Park, it's going to cost more) and if it was available, we'd call Bob. And he'd tell us it was gone.

One listing came available while we were out on our search. Bob told us the building was on 74th and 1st. I noticed right away that there was a Bodega on the ground floor, with flowers lining the outside. That made me feel welcome, and the neighborhood also had a nice, sort of friendly feel.

We went inside and climbed to the 4th floor. By this point, I had sweat through my clothes and my legs were cramping up from all the stairs. I was so tired, sticky, and probably stinky that I wanted to sit on the step and yell up for someone to open the door and send down a picture. Wishful thinking on my part, of course. I could tell Jerusalem's ball of energy was shrinking as well. He wiped a bead of perspiration from his forehead and started up the next level of stairs. I followed reluctantly.

We finally made it up the remaining two flights of stairs and went inside the apartment. I was surprised. It was by far the best we'd seen all day. There was usually an oddity in each place we'd seen, though this one trumped the rest. There was a wall in the middle of the apartment that was sort of triangle-shaped and jutted out, so you had to squeeze by it no matter where you went in the apartment. I squeezed by it when we headed to the kitchen. *Was the wall trying to eat me?*

Beyond that feature, I liked it. I asked Jerusalem to call Bob.

It was gone.

Strange, because I had a good feeling about that building,

as if I was sure that was where I was going to live. We went outside and sat on the steps to regroup. Jerusalem's big, brimming smile from that morning had now become a look of concern, but he stayed optimistic.

"We'll find you something today. I know it," he said.

We went to the upper west side and looked at a few more weird triangle-shaped apartments. They didn't have walls in the middle of them like the previous apartment, they were just triangle-shaped in general. I wondered where I could find furniture angled to match the corners of an isosceles triangle - was there a store for that?

On the way out, Jerusalem got a call from Bob. An apartment had opened up at that building back on 74th and 1st.

So we got back on the train and traveled across town. My clothes had given up under the pressure of the 90 degree heat and humidity, and now clung to me like a soggy second skin. I wanted to run and jump in the East River.

We arrived at the corner of 74th and 1st. The flowers that lined the bodega were like a welcome home present, that was until Jerusalem said the available apartment was on the 6th floor. I think I actually *heard* my legs groan at the anticipation of climbing those stairs one more time.

After hauling my stinky, tired ass up those 80 steps, I could barely bring myself to touch the doorknob - not in fear that it might fall off, but out of sheer exhaustion. I quickly pushed open the door, and that's when I heard the heavens open up and the "Aaaaaaah!" of angels as I entered. It was bright and cheery, with windows that nearly went from floor to ceiling - and the ceilings were high! There was even a window in the bathroom. I looked at the apartment for all of 30 seconds before I blurted out, "Call Bob!"

The apartment was available - that was the first step. Even though it was over the $800 budget I initially wanted to spend a month - it was $1525 per month - it was perfect. Besides, who needs to eat?

I come from a middle-class family, so we know the value of a dollar. When I said yes to this apartment, I had $5,000 saved and thought that would be enough for a first month's rent and security.

In New York, that kind of money is a meal and a show. So, when I got back to the agency with Jerusalem, Bob was trying to get me to sign over my savings, my next of kin, and seal the deal with my kidney. Not really, but close.

I was terrified.

At one point, Bob was yelling (or I guess talking in his regular voice) at me to call my bank. He needed the balance in my savings account for the paper work we had to fill out.

Then, after all that paperwork was finished, he said, "Oh wait, you're a graduate student. You can't get an apartment without a co-signer."

I wanted to fling myself out the window. This meant asking my parents to co-sign. Not good. My father had specifically said to me before I left, "Don't ask us for any money."

Not that I had been planning on it, but now what was I supposed to do? Again, the green, clueless girl from Wisconsin had no idea it would be this hard to get an apartment in New York. And to need a co-signer? I'd never heard of that policy.

In Wisconsin, people practically gave you the keys to their house for free.

I looked at Bob, whose nostrils were flared with his face red and flushed, and I thought he was ready to pick up his desk and throw it at me.

I turned around to find Jerusalem, who came over to us with his kind energy. "Why don't you get a payment to hold it while she talks to her parents, Bob?"

Thank you, Jerusalem.

I gave Bob a down payment of one month's rent and security. I called and talked to Mom, who thankfully agreed.

Bob faxed the paperwork to my parents, and I left with an apartment and an ulcer.

Chapter Eight

I'm Not in Wisconsin Anymore

While I waited at the airport for my flight, I got a call from Bob, who surprisingly sounded so much sweeter on the phone. Perhaps, it was because he got his money. He told me that my parents' paperwork checked out. They could be my co-signers. I had the apartment. *Fabulous.*

Then he suggested we get a drink together some time after I moved to the city. I tried to imagine how much alcohol I'd have to ingest to allow myself to relax around Bob and his Tony Soprano-ish personality.

Upon landing in Milwaukee, I stepped off the plane and felt a bit like a hermit crab trying to shove myself back into my old shell. I'd done what I thought was impossible. One of the hardest parts of the move was finding an apartment and I could cross that off my list. I was brimming with a confidence I'd never had before, and now, I could concentrate on getting to *grad* school.

Shortly after I returned home, I got my reading list in the mail. It was quite extensive.

When my brother stopped by to see me, I showed it to him. I was surprised by the length of the list.

My older brother said, "Well, Erin, you are going to grad school."

Oh yea, right.

There wasn't much to do after that. I was done working at the PAC, I sold my furniture, and I purchased a purple suitcase the size of a small car. Even still, it was hard to condense my entire life into one bag. It was like appearing on a reverse episode of the Hoarders. I never knew I would have such a tough time letting go of tchotchkes like a candle in the shape of Buddha that my younger brother gave me, or a ceramic shoe that was my grandmother's. It wasn't what the items represented. I think it was more the fear that none of the items could go with me, and neither could the people who gave them to me. I shared my dilemma with Mom as I sat on the living room floor with my three-year-old niece, Maggie, tossing a rubber, glow-in-the-dark ball back and forth. Mom told me to make a "ship" pile of things that she could mail to me later.

So, I was ready to go, and I was scared to death.

* * *

Then the big day came - August 16th. I had been staying at my parents' house after my lease was up. I hugged them good-bye inside the house, but Mom followed me out to the car.

I'll never forget the look on her face. It was the first time I was moving out of the state. I had lived all over Wisconsin, but never anywhere outside of its borders. Mom stood there watching me as I pulled out of the driveway. I blinked quickly to fight back the tears - it was Mom who had stepped up when I needed help with the apartment. Mom who was shipping things to me, Mom who told me I could do it. She was always in my corner and I was so grateful to her. I wanted to do well, not just for myself but for her, too.

I drove to Appleton in Grandmother's car to my older brother's house. They were out of town, but Josie was picking me up there after work. Together, we were driving to her brother's house in Milwaukee. We'd stay overnight there, and she'd drop me off at the airport in the morning. That seemed a good way to transition - I had said my good-byes to everyone and I could focus on what lay ahead.

Of course, I couldn't sleep that night. I was awake before the alarm went off. Josie and I talked while she drove - the weather was rainy and humid. When we got to the airport, she came in with me. I hate good-byes. Saying good-bye to her was like saying good-bye to a sister. She was one of the best friends I'd ever had and I knew our relationship would change.

I started to tear up and then so did she, so I hugged her and said, "I'm not going to say good-bye. I'll see you again soon."

"You're going to be great, Erin," she said.

Then I turned and headed to the security check point.

The three times I'd been to New York previously I'd felt excited, not scared. This time when the plane landed, I felt as if I had a cannon ball on my chest. I wasn't visiting - I was moving there.

Reality hit me hard. *How did this happen?*

As I got off the plane - it was incredibly hot and humid, and again, I was wearing clothes that were way too warm - I looked at my phone to find the email from Bob. It told me where the rental office was located so I could pick up the keys to the apartment. I stood in line waiting for a cab, remembering in my head to tell the cabby the cross streets. The rental agency was near my apartment on 3rd and 77th.

After I got out of the cab with my enormous suitcase, I stepped through the doorway and looked up at the three flights of marble stairs. I debated what to do, and realized I had to lug the suitcase up the stairs with me. I felt like Lucille Ball, wishing Ethel Mertz was there to help me. The suitcase weighed over 50 pounds, and although I was strong, there were a few moments when I wondered if I'd fall backwards down the stairs. I didn't want to have to start over again.

On the third floor, I stepped through the glass door and the receptionist looked at me much like the real estate receptionist had looked at me months ago. I probably looked wide-eyed and terrified.

As I approached her, I told her I was there to pick up my key, but she didn't know anything about it.

This scared me. I mentioned Bob's name from the agency and she told me to wait a minute. She headed through another glass door behind her.

I sat down to wait and could hear a man on the phone say, "We had a break-in last night. Can you go there and change the locks?"

The receptionist came back and said, "Paul will see you in a minute so you can sign your lease. Why didn't you come and sign it sooner?"

"I wasn't in the state."

I figured Bob had set this all up for me because he said he had. What other surprises lay in store?

I met with Paul, and he seemed like a less scarier version of Bob. He had me sign my life away and told me he didn't know if he could give me the keys to the apartment today because he didn't know if the previous tenants were out.

I explained that I had moved from Wisconsin, just landing in New York today. I didn't have anywhere else to go. I sat there sweating, wondering what I had done. Would I be homeless on my first night?

He left to speak with the receptionist. After several long minutes, he finally returned and told me that they'd get a hold of the superintendent to see if I could move in today.

I thanked him and sat in the lobby, trying to figure out what to do if I couldn't get into the apartment. What were my options? I could stay in a hotel, but for how long and where?

As I sat there trying not to panic, I texted Tara. I thought if I could see a friendly face, perhaps it would keep me calm.

She texted back immediately. She asked where I was and messaged that she'd meet me.

I waited in the office for an hour before they came out and gave me the keys. *Whew!*

Tara came in, and I wanted to hug her - I was so happy to see her.

We lugged my suitcase down the stairs and headed toward the apartment. She knew exactly where to go, so I followed her.

She was stunning, wearing an adorable sundress. I wore a shirt that I had already sweat through twice and a pair of knit shorts. Why I thought that had been the right thing to wear that day was beyond reasoning.

We made it to my new apartment building and I smiled

when I saw the flowers in front. We found the main door and I tried the key, which didn't seem to work.

The superintendent came around the corner to let me know the apartment was ready. He told me to try the lock again - that it was tricky. I did, and it finally opened.

We made our way through the hallway and up the six flights of stairs to the top. Tara was a dear and gave me a short break. She carried my suitcase up one of the flights of stairs, but I felt guilty letting her, so I took it back.

On the 6th floor, I stood gasping for breath. I wanted to peel my clothes off and take a cold shower. I looked at Tara and she looked fresh as a daisy.

Again, I struggled with the key. Tara asked if she could give it a try, and she had the magic touch. The door swung open.

I looked around. This didn't look like the same place I had seen a month ago. I had seen it with furniture in it. Jerusalem had mentioned that it helped to see a place when it's furnished because it made the place seem homier. He was right. It looked like an empty hallway.

Tara's jaw dropped. "Wow, this is big. You'll have to come see our apartment. It's so much smaller."

When I heard that, it put things into perspective for me. I was lucky to have found that special apartment. I'd make it my home. There was no dresser, so I stood my luggage in a corner to open later.

Tara said she'd show me the way to NYU on the subway and we could stop at Kmart to pick up a few things, like an air

     Dorothy Never Got Down Like This

mattress for me to sleep on until I could get furniture.

We walked to Lexington and 77th and went down into the subway. We got on the 6 train, and it was crowded (as the 6 train usually is) so we stood.

I didn't grab onto anything, and just as Tara was telling me to, the train took off.

I went flying.

Tara turned her back to me, probably because it was hilarious. This happens to nearly every first-timer standing on the subway. It is the mark of a New York newbie.

I laughed at myself and stood up, grabbing the pole. I heard the stop for 'Astor Place' and we got out, seeing the entrance to Kmart at the end of the subway platform.

We went inside, and Tara and I found an air mattress, sheets, and a few other essentials I needed. We checked out and returned to the subway.

We stopped at the library to use the computers, so I could order furniture. Silly me, for not doing that ahead of time and thinking it wouldn't take long.

I clicked onto a furniture website and tried ordering a futon. Every incoming NYU student was probably doing the same thing right then, so the only ones left were the funky-colored ones. I chose a hunter green covered futon. It wasn't as bad as the picture made it look.

"Three weeks?" I said, shocked. I wouldn't have a bed to sleep on for three weeks.

Tara said that was normal and reminded me that

everything took more time in New York.

We arrived back home at my new place, and I thanked Tara for all her help. She hugged me, and then I watched her walk away. The only friendly face I knew in New York, besides her boyfriend. I wanted to run after her and grab her, not letting go.

She disappeared around the corner and I realized I was all alone. I felt a knot in my throat. I swallowed hard and headed upstairs to the apartment.

I opened the door and ran my fingers through my hair, sighing as my eyes fell on that purple suitcase in the middle of my apartment. It was staring back at me like a kid who I'd left at the bus station. I walked up to it, kicked it over with my foot and unzipped the top when my niece, Maggie's glow-in-the-dark rubber ball popped out.

"Oh!" I chirped as tears rolled down my cheeks. I remembered she had walked down the hall in my parents' house that day with the ball and came back to the living room without it, empty-handed. It never occurred to me that a three-year-old would somehow think to put it in my suitcase. I picked it up and bounced it on the bare hardwood floors, smiling. She'd sent a piece of home with me.

That night I lay on the floor on my air mattress. It was at least 90 degrees in the apartment. I was sweating and there was a noise I couldn't identify coming from outside the window. It never stopped, it just got louder. It was coming from a ventilation shaft along the building.

I tried to tune out the hum from outside as I laid there in the dark, sweating, hoping I didn't have cockroaches. I wanted to cry.

Don't cry. One day, you will look on this as the best time of your life.

Chapter Nine

Off to See the Wizard (otherwise known as NYU)

The next day when I awoke I decided to head down to NYU, spend some time in the library and knock out some of those plays on my reading list.

I showered - even though it was 96 degrees and 100 percent humidity, which is always lovely because when you step out of the shower, you dry off and you're wet again in 2.3 seconds. Before I dressed, I did the Laverne and Shirley thing and stood in front of my refrigerator and freezer with the doors open, trying to cool off. (*Laverne and Shirley* was a TV show that aired in the late 1970s about two roommates based in Milwaukee.) I wiped myself down with a towel for the fifteenth time and fanned myself before getting dressed, which reminded me a bit of an animal in a zoo, but whatever. I pulled on my sundress and some flats, grabbed my purse, and headed out into the city.

I took a moment to acclimate myself to my surroundings. Everything still seemed foreign to me - as if at any moment a tornado would come along and plop me back in the Dairy State.

I remembered where the subway was and headed in that direction. I walked leisurely, taking in the buildings and landmarks that lined the streets, so as to familiarize myself with the neighborhoods. There was a pleasant August breeze that tickled my cheeks - I'm kidding, that was just in my head. The "animal in a zoo" feeling continued as sweat ran

 Dorothy Never Got Down Like This

down my back, and I realized I probably should've brought deodorant with me - another thing to remember in New York in summer. Don't leave home without your water bottle and your deodorant.

When I got to 77th and Lexington, I went down into the subway, making sure to get on the downtown train, not the uptown train - something Jerusalem mentioned to me while we were apartment hunting. I was lucky. The train was just arriving, so I jumped on.

I grabbed an open pole and the train jolted forward. I looked at all the different faces, people of all different ages from all different places standing in the car. I loved that about New York - people coming together from all over the world, living in one place. What could be more serendipitous? When the train jolted forward and I didn't feel like a drunk person on a treadmill, I smiled. I had found my footing. *I'm doing this. By myself.* I had been so afraid of using the subways and learning the trains, but I knew once I did it alone, it would get easier.

I heard the barely audible voice of the announcer bark "Astor Place" and remembered that was my stop. I leapt off the train, almost wanting to break into a sprint. I was so excited to be a part of NYU. I was practically skipping as I watched for the purple flag that said Tisch School of the Arts.

When I saw the building and the cursive writing that said TISCH, it was like seeing the Mother ship. I stood under the flag and stared up, still in disbelief. I'd be attending my dream school in less than two weeks. *Amazing!*

Across the street was the bookstore. My first stop.

I stepped inside and saw another amazing sight - an

incredibly handsome man - segue here, my first few days in New York I'd been seeing them everywhere. I'd come to some magical world where every man was tall, dark, handsome, and oozing sexuality.

He smiled. "Can I help you find something?"

Ah, yes, a new pair of panties please. He was the first person to speak to me since I left Tara in the street the day before.

"I'm attending Tisch next semester and - "

He interrupted, "What program?"

"The Graduate Musical Theatre Writing Program," I said.

"Really? I'm in that program." He nearly leapt over the counter to give me a hug. His embrace was so warm and genuine I wanted to linger all day.

I don't think I'd ever hugged a man who was that well-formed. It was like embracing the statue of David. He leaned back and met my eyes again. He had jet-black hair and clear blue eyes, traits that reminded me of my first love. He said his name was Jason and that he was in the second year of the program.

Serendipity? I bombarded him with questions; how much time would we have to write a song? Would I have to sing in front of people, blah, blah, blah... That's when he patted me on the shoulder and told me to take a deep breath.

"Don't worry, Erin. You'll be fine, but the first year is a little like boot camp."

Ugh, boot camp. What did that mean?

Jason and I talked a bit more before I did a quick circle and left the store. I was so happy I'd met him. It was exciting to think that on the first day, there would be at least one familiar face.

I made my way to the library. As I went through the doors I stood frozen, looking up in awe. The center of the library has an open foyer all the way to the top floor. It was a beautiful sight.

I stepped forward to go through the gate, but I was stopped by a security officer. Silly Wisconsin girl, thinks she can walk into any place without identification.

"Do you have your ID?" she asked.

I started to take out my driver's license, but I didn't think that's what she meant. "Ah, no," I said. "What do you mean?"

"You need a student ID to get in."

"Okay," I said, "where do I get that?"

She gave me directions, which went in my head and out like water through a sieve. I stepped out of the library and looked around, trying to recall what she had told me.

When I finally figured it out, I noticed there was a line.

It only took a few minutes before my photo was taken and my ID was printed. I saw my picture and cringed. It was the first time the picture didn't match the person I was becoming. My hair was short and in that crappy in-between stage because I was trying to grow it out. I was sweaty and overweight - something I'd struggled with my entire life.

Because of my obsession with *The Wizard of Oz*, I also had

an obsession with Judy Garland. I would lie in bed at night and quietly sing "Somewhere over the Rainbow" in hopes that if I practiced enough I would one day do it justice. I never could hit those notes quite like Miss Garland, though.

I read about how she was treated as a child actor. She signed a contract with MGM when she was just thirteen. While it's said that Louis B. Mayer signed her almost immediately after hearing her sing, he also immediately became the food police, controlling everything she ate and was allowed to eat while filming. And since they were filming for 14-16 hours a day, Judy wasn't able to eat much. Her diet was said to consist of chicken soup, black coffee, and cigarettes. The idea of doing this to a thirteen-year-old girl makes me want to go back in time and pelt these people with soup cans, but I digress.

Which brings me to why I'm telling you this. I could relate to Judy's story because I had a similar situation. Growing up in my family, Dad ate like a wolf, so my brothers followed suit, and unless I wanted to starve, I had to jump in there and grab my meal with the best of them.

I remember being a happy child and never really thinking there was anything wrong with me until about age ten. I was always tall and never petite, but again, that never seemed to bother me all that much. That was until I turned into a teenager. Note to teenagers – don't believe that there is anything wrong with you. You are perfect the way you are – absolutely perfect – God made you that way.

I wish someone would have told me that back then. When I was a Freshman in high school, I stopped eating. I don't mean that I didn't eat much. I mean, I stopped eating. The only time I'd eat was when I couldn't stand the hunger anymore. Then, I would eat *half* of an apple or a *piece* of lettuce. I became a rabbit.

When I ate something substantial, I would throw it up. It didn't occur to me that I had an eating disorder. I thought I was fine until someone at school noticed how much weight I'd lost.

Then one of my brother's friends noticed, saying "Erin, you're starting to look a bit waifish." Waifish had never been a word used to describe me before.

I thought I was starting to look a bit skeletal and I wanted to eat everything in sight - I could've eaten the sole of my shoe at that point - anything sounded good. Even though I wanted to eat, I couldn't. I had twisted my relationship with food from eating too much too fast to eating nothing, ever. Neither of which were healthy.

Then my parents realized what was happening.

After seeing our family doctor, it was recommended to them that they take me to Madison to an outpatient clinic for people with eating disorders.

What? Me? Eating disorder? I was too ordinary to have an eating disorder.

But I did.

I had symptoms of both anorexia and bulimia - this is how indecisive of a person I am. I was binging and purging so they treated me for bulimia. The treatment focused on helping me recognize the damage that was being done to my body and helped me correct my relationship with food.

While there, I met other women in the clinic. They scared me straight. Some of the girls' hair was falling out, others had teeth that were rotting due to the acid that erodes your gums from vomiting. I saw how horrifying this epidemic was first hand and realized I wanted to be an example of health - at whatever weight my body decided was right for me. The doctors and the nutritionists at the clinic helped me do that.

The thing that struck me the most at the end of my treatment was what one of the nurses said to me, "You'll always have these symptoms. It's knowing how to manage them."

I still struggle with my weight. As a woman, I think we have to condition ourselves to be happy with who we are, exactly the way we are, no apologies. God knows there'll always be someone who can't wait to make you feel bad about yourself because they're insecure. I refuse to allow anyone else's opinion to affect me anymore because it's *their* image of me, not mine.

These feelings still creep in and I still find myself stressed when my jeans get too tight. But now I write about it. Often it ends up in a stand-up routine somewhere, that's an outlet that works for me.

Chapter Ten

I'm Not in Wisconsin Anymore

The next two weeks I filled my time sitting in the NYU library reading musicals and plays, crossing them off my list.

I have to admit, those weeks before grad school started were lonely. I had never been in a place where I didn't have someone I knew close by. The furthest I'd moved away from my family was to Madison, about 180 miles away, but *this* was a whole new experience. Not to mention the heat and humidity were unrelenting in New York.

I stood washing my clothes in my kitchen sink one day. As I was scrubbing them, I looked out the window at the brick wall across from me. I hadn't talked to anyone in days. I hadn't heard from Tara. The reality of where I was living was settling in, and I started sobbing. I reminded myself I was starting school soon and that excited me. I went downstairs to the bodega and talked to the clerk for about an hour. Luis and I were becoming best friends.

Besides Luis, there was a door-sitter in front of my building. He was a homeless guy who hung out on the doorstep and asked everyone to buy him whiskey and cigarettes. My door-sitter's name was Warren, and I grew quite attached to him.

When I came to New York for the first time, I had been with Mom and my grandparents. I was sixteen. We had eaten in a fancy restaurant and I was sitting there at our table with my doggie bag - what I had not eaten was more than enough for two people - when I saw a man standing in the doorway. I had been watching him through the window. He had been lingering outside the building. It seemed as if he was struggling to stand, not as if he was drunk, but it appeared as if he was weak. His tattered coat hung on him and almost looked as if it was weighing him down. His hair was matted and clung to his cheeks, meeting an unkempt beard. While he appeared gentle and harmless, the look of hunger on his face was clear - like a starving lion waiting to pounce on its prey. He was disheveled and could barely speak. The host asked if he could help him. I observed the man as he barely squeaked out, "To eat."

The host then threw the man out of the restaurant.

I sat there, staring at my doggie bag, wanting so much to run out into the street and hand it to him. But I didn't. Why *didn't* I? That moment stuck with me, though. It was the moment when I realized how much I had and how blessed I was to have my family and friends.

So, when I moved into my apartment in Manhattan and met Warren, I felt blessed. Warren was always there to greet me as I arrived home with a big hug and a sloppy kiss on the cheek that was more like a greeting from a puppy than a person. I didn't mind it. I started to think of him as family - after all, he was part of this new life in New York. He started to learn that, while I wouldn't buy him alcohol or cigarettes, I would occasionally bring him a sandwich or water. Often times, he would remind me, "I like ham, girl." So, ham it was.

The first day of orientation came. I was so nervous. It was also the same day that my furniture arrived.

I didn't realize the delivery service charged per floor. I was on the 6th floor. They said that would be an extra $300. Well,

    Dorothy Never Got Down Like This

hmmm, that's more than the entire cost of the hideous green futon. I whined enough that the guy only charged me $50 to bring it up the six flights of stairs.

I now had a mattress and a frame - which needed to be assembled. I plopped down in the middle of my apartment, took the plastic off of it, and two gigantic horse flies flew out. From their reaction, they'd been in that plastic for a long time. They buzzed around the apartment.

Meanwhile, I took the frame out of the box, read the instructions, and laughed. *I may be sleeping on the air mattress tonight.*

No, I had to make this work. I summoned all my patience and put the frame together. When I was finished, I admitted I was proud of myself. I'd done it. Now, on to the next challenge - NYU.

After assembling my furniture, I realized I'd be in my first class at Tisch in less than 24 hours. I swallowed hard. I ignored the fact that I was sweating profusely because it was still 96 degrees outside with 100% humidity. There were so many things about moving to New York that terrified me, but the scariest of all was the reality that I was *actually* attending grad school at NYU.

I had gone through all the steps to make it possible and now that it was about to be real, I felt paralyzed. What if I was terrible? What if I couldn't write? What if I couldn't keep up with the pace? What if I had a professor that didn't like me? My brain wouldn't stop creating worse-case scenarios.

The next day I dressed in an outfit I hoped I wouldn't sweat through. The humidity was like that annoying person that never leaves a party. I kept wondering when there would be some relief. I made my way to the subway with my stomach in knots. When the 6 train stopped at Astor Place, I debated getting out. I wanted to run back to my apartment and hide under the futon. *How could I do this?*

I pushed myself forward. I had to do this for me. I exited the train and made my way to Broadway. Luckily, all the time I spent on campus weeks before the program had started helped me get familiar with it. I saw the purple flag above the door that read Tisch School of the Arts and I stepped inside.

I had received an email that requested we all meet on the 12th floor in the Dean's office before classes began because the building that housed our program was under construction. I didn't know where the Dean's office was, so I looked for signs directing me. I went into the elevator, hit 12, and waited.

Elevators freak me out. The idea of riding in a heavy, metal box that's dangling by a cable is disturbing. I debated taking the stairs but laughed at myself, remembering the 80 steps I had to climb to get into my apartment.

The elevator stopped, and I heard the ding as the doors flung open. I wanted to melt into the floor or become a vapor that could escape out a window.

I saw a receptionist desk in front of me. There was a hum of activity happening, and I knew as soon as I stepped off the elevator I would be a part of it. For me, it was the moment the house landed and Dorothy stepped out into Technicolor. I wished for someone to be there to guide me.

I stepped forward and timidly asked the administrative assistant where the Dean's office was. She gave me a beaming smile and kindly pointed me in the right direction.

I walked down the hall, hoping to turn invisible when I saw an enormous office with glass doors that lined the front of it. I could see clear through the office to the Empire State Building behind it. It was set perfectly in the middle of the window as if the NYU building was designed with that in mind.

My eyes widened and my mouth dropped as I felt someone's gaze on me. I looked up.

A young man with spectacles smiled at me and said, "Are you here for the musical theatre writing program?"

"I am." I returned his smile.

"I'm Tres."

As I shook Tres' hand, a short, younger-looking girl with bib-overalls came up behind us. Her hair was cut to frame her strong features. I looked at her, with my first thought being, *we're going to be good friends.*

"Hey, I'm Lee."

"Hi, Lee," I said.

While Tres, Lee, and I stood awkwardly trying to hide our nerves, one-by-one people arrived in the hallway. Even as adults, cliques were being formed. I looked for the group I might fit into, but there was no slightly dorky, Midwestern group.

That was, until I met Clay.

I don't think I've ever met anyone who I immediately felt I understood until I met Clay. He was tall and looked like a young Shaun Cassidy, which is a reference a little even before my time. Cassidy was a TV star with a one-hit wonder in the late 1970s. He also had incredible hair.

Clay came up behind me and introduced himself.

I said something, and it sent him into hysterics - he was holding his stomach. When he recovered, he smiled and said, "You're my new best friend."

And from then on, he was the Scarecrow to my Dorothy.

Once all 32 of my fellow classmates arrived - the largest class in the history of the musical theatre writing program - the glass doors swung open. As we filed into the room, the cycle before us, Cycle 20 cheered and applauded us! They waved and hollered for us to come on in and then, their voices culminated into a cheer of welcome. What a way to be greeted into the program!

I looked around the room and realized how stunning the class was - not to mention how attractive the people in my cycle were.

In the class ahead of us there was a tall, willowy red head with a voice like a lark. Jason - the hunky guy I'd met earlier in the book store. There was a unique, Erika Badu type woman with glasses and an adorable squeak of a laugh, and Masayu. When Masayu introduced himself and said he was from Wisconsin, it immediately made me feel close to him.

It wasn't until he sang that everything below my waist went weak. Oh, dear God, how could a man's voice do that to my body? *Wow!* I had my first Tisch crush.

We watched and listened as Cycle 20 shared their work with us. I sat stunned. *How in God's name could I produce work like theirs?* Really? As each person came up to sing and present a song, I was fixed on them, wondering how I would be able to come up with something nearly as good.

After the concert, Cycle 20 invited us to a bar on St. Mark's Place, an historic street in the city near NYU. I went out with the group, trying to appear calm and collected. Clay and I walked together, chatting with other people. Masayu happened to be near me, so I introduced myself and told him where I was from. He had an enigmatic, warm smile and kind eyes.

I observed the campus atmosphere fall away and the village atmosphere take over. There was a feeling of energy and creativity - or at least it seemed that way to me.

We arrived in front of the bar, which led downstairs underground. A lot of bars and restaurants that lined the streets were like this, and I loved the feel of it - as if they were hidden away like speakeasies.

Inside, it was dark and the ceilings were low like it was some sexy hideaway. Everyone intermingled and introduced themselves, also saying where they were from. Clay was from Peoria, Illinois, Lee was from Atlanta, Georgia, and Tres was from California. Four students had come from Seoul, Korea, and a hulking, lovable Norwegian named Godtfred was part of the class. Others had come from all over the country - Michigan, Washington, North Carolina, and Texas.

The women in my cycle were stunning. Scarlet and Betty were both from New York, and this woman, Beth, who was from Texas, was so beautiful. I didn't want to stand near her for fear of becoming invisible. Ruth came from California and the straight men were already fighting over her. And then there was this incredibly quiet, gorgeous woman named Sandra. Amidst all these talented, beautiful people I felt incredibly inadequate, not worthy of breathing the same air.

I was much older than most of them in my cycle. Me being thirty-seven and most of the students under twenty-five. I was drawn to the students in cycle 20 who were closer to my age. I met Maria and connected with her. She was near my age and had an incredible laugh.

After a few hours, things wound down. I made my way back to the subway with Clay, Lee, Tres, Godtfred, and a few others. As we were saying our good-byes, I looked around and realized where I lived. It was stunning to me.

Clay gave me a hug and said he'd see me tomorrow. That's when I realized this was the start of my bewitching journey that would become the best time of my life thus far.

Chapter Eleven

The Good Witch

The next day I returned to the Tisch Gates. My classmates and I had been instructed to meet there early, with the faculty letting us know there was a surprise for us. A surprise? Really? *How much better could things get?* This is what I asked myself when I woke up that morning.

I made my way back to the 12th floor, still stunned by the view of the Empire State building and strolled through the stately glass doors. I noticed there was a buzz in the air, which seemed to double the excitement from the day before. I looked about for Clay, when someone's hand gently nudged my shoulder. It was Tres.

"Did you hear?" he said, wide-eyed.

"Hear what?" I asked.

"Winnie Holzman. She's coming. Any minute."

WHAT? I nearly leaped out of my skin. *The* Winnie Holzman was coming to talk to us. Not only was Winnie Holzman my writing hero, she was also a big part of the reason I applied to Tisch. I remember falling in love with her television drama series that she wrote in the 90s called *My So-Called Life.*

Winnie is most known for writing the book (script) for that little-known musical titled *Wicked.* Regardless, I was off-the-charts excited that we would meet her. The chair of the department had told us the day before during introductions that Winnie was an alumni of our program, and she was always willing to pop in to meet the new students in their first year and later hear their thesis ideas in year two.

I found a seat next to Tres and was still scanning the room for Clay when I heard my phone beep. He had texted to say his doorknob fell off on his apartment door and he was trapped. Apparently, door knobs falling off of New York apartments wasn't uncommon. I texted him that I would let the faculty know. He was trying desperately to get a hold of his landlord to let him out of his 14th floor studio.

I tucked my phone into my pocket and as I did, the glass doors swung open. In came Laura, the chair of the department, followed by Winnie Holzman.

Winnie was a tiny woman with jet black hair and a convivial demeanor. Laura introduced Winnie - as if she needed any introduction - and Winnie started by telling us a little about her experience in the program, which went a little something like this:

"I was in Cycle 1, back when we made music with steam."

The room filled with laughter as she immediately put us all at ease. She went on to talk about projects she was working on, and then she took questions from us. I was too star struck to ask any, but the one thing she said that resonated with me was when she was asked if things got any easier regarding pursuing a career as a writer.

She paused for a moment and took a breath. "Well, I don't like the word *easy*. Because none of this is easy," she said. "You know you'll always be working with someone; a collaborator, actors, if you want to write books, an editor, so none of this is ever easy. It's hard work."

And little did I know how right she was. I had no idea of the work that was yet to come for me. I was about to be my own worst enemy during my first semester at Tisch.

* * *

After Winnie's presentation, the class was given our first tasks, one of which included a scavenger hunt planned by Cycle 20 that took us throughout the NYU campus, Union square, and the East Village. We divided up into teams and had a list of things we had to seek out. I understand it was in an effort to learn the campus and the part of the city it was in, but Cycle 20 didn't make it easy on us.

It was one of those sweltering summer days in New York City. The kind that makes you wish you were on a front porch somewhere in the country with a fan and a mint julep. We went off with our teams, and after about two hours of searching for clues, I was ready to stop for some refreshment. Maybe not a mint julep, but a big beer would've been nice.

It just so happened one of our stops was at a bar. It was the White Horse Tavern, which is known for lively conversations with Dylan Thomas and other well-known writers beginning in the 1950s - a very fitting place for a bunch of budding writers to stop. When I realized that, my thirst for a beer went away as I closed my eyes and imagined Thomas sitting at the bar, smoking a cigar, and talking to other writers about their latest projects. Perhaps the more alcohol they consumed, the more ideas came tumbling out through the smoke. I placed my hands on the cushion of a bar stool and spun it around, wondering if it was where Dylan Thomas himself may have sat.

With a tap on the shoulder, I snapped out of my fantasy, seeing the lovely, dark-haired Sabrina with the husky alto voice I so admired behind me. She was wearing Doc Martens and lifting her feet as if she had bricks tied to them. I could tell she was exhausted.

I offered her the stool I had been spinning, and she sat down. I took a seat next to her when we noticed some of our comrades from Cycle 20 down at the other end of the bar having a beer. With a quick "cheers," they held up their glasses to us and reminded us not to sit too long. It was a race after all.

With that, we regrouped and headed back out into the heat. As I walked to the door I brushed my finger over the woodwork, as if trying to soak in something for good luck.

We stumbled to NYU, clammy and sticky and wanting to jump in the Washington Square park fountain. We arrived back on the 12th floor, as construction was still going on in what would prove to be our regular space at Tisch. While everyone whirled around the room, I took a seat near the window and peered out at the Empire State building. I took a moment to pay attention to my breath, my heartbeat. I had to let it sink in. I was now living in the place of my dreams and going to bars where people like Dylan Thomas and Bob Dylan had hung out. I listened to my heartbeat and breathed in the energy of the talented people in the room whom I would soon call friends. I memorized the image of the Empire State Building, which would become my beacon on so many different occasions, both of success, failure, and even pain. I took it all in at that moment and knew I was exactly where I was supposed to be.

That lasted for about two wonderful, momentous seconds, until my insecurities took over and I realized I was in a room with incredibly TALENTED people and I was going to have to try to produce work worthy of being at Tisch. My thoughts started to turn in on me. I could hear that old familiar track playing in my head telling me I should run out the door now, grab a block of cheese on the way, and hide in my apartment until the two years were over.

Well, I didn't do that. What I did do was continue to observe the energy in the room. Everyone was beautiful and talented. *Have I mentioned talented?* And I felt, well, I felt not beautiful or talented. It was one of those moments that I look back on and wish I could've snapped out of it. There were so many things I wouldn't do on a social level while in grad school because I let my insecurities get the better of me.

Don't do that when you're chasing your dream. Soak in everything, do everything, and be loving to everyone - and let the chips fall where they may.

Next, we were given our first song assignment. I had spent most of my life making up songs in my head, singing to myself, jotting down a lyric here and there, but had never actually attempted to write a complete lyric. I applied to Tisch knowing that songwriting was one of the skills I wanted to learn. Most of the people in my cycle had visited the school in March the year prior for applicants' weekend. I had missed it because I was still working and busy filling out the rest of the application. Had I been at applicants' weekend I think it would've made the next part of the process a little easier for me.

We were paired up and given a prompt to write a song. My partner was Dylan - this tall, hunky blond guy from Michigan. I couldn't spend a lot of time talking to him without thinking about tearing off his clothes. I don't know if this came with age or lack of sex, but I was certainly suffering from both.

The prompt Dylan and I received was Dolly Parton. Not knowing what to do with that, he and I met to talk about ideas, then we went our separate ways. I told him I would email him with what I had as soon as possible because we only had 24 hours to come up with something.

I went home to my apartment and thought about Dolly Parton. (There's a sentence you don't read every day.) I wrote a line, then deleted it. I jotted down an idea, then crossed it out. I came up with a rhyme. *They'll think it will suck.*

Hours flew by and I had nothing to pass on to Dylan. This was bad. And what I did come up with was so bad I'm not going to include it in this book.

I can only guess Dylan read that email and then flopped his head down on the piano keys, wondering why he got stuck with me as a partner. That lyric - or whatever you want to call it, (how about crap?) hurts my head to think about it now, knowing that's what I passed off to him.

It doesn't get any better, either. Dylan wasn't all that inspired by that poopy lyric. Could you blame him? He didn't compose many lines of music to it, so when we showed up the next morning to perform our song for faculty (GULP), I didn't know it was going to be as painful as it was.

I thought everyone was going to write bits and pieces of something. That there would be a sense of "hey, this is a start, but it's not perfect." Nope! Everyone came with their A-game.

Our lovable Norwegian, Godtfred, and Scarlet - who was stunning without singing a note, got up in front of the class. Godtfred pounded out an upbeat, jazzy rhythm and Scarlet sang about her Acupuncturist and how he turned her on. It was hilarious. She whipped her long, auburn locks around while singing "My Acu-Puncture-ist" and practically having an orgasm on stage with the funny lyrics she wrote.

I sat with my jaw in my lap - we were screwed! I started to wonder if they would send me home after hearing my song.

After Scarlet and Godtfred, everyone who went up afterwards hit a lyrical home run. I was sinking in my seat. *Dear God, what was I doing at Tisch? Could I jump out of this 12th story window and run for the airport? FUCK!*

Finally, Dylan and I decided to get it over with. We slogged our way up to the piano. Oh yeah, the other thing is, I don't sing, so that also made for part of our dilemma.

As I stood there trying to fake confidence, I could feel Laura's eyes on me. Sitting beside Laura was Dill, a red-headed adjunct professor who had gone to Harvard and had written a book of poetry, which was very well-received by the outside world. I hadn't seen him before, but he appeared hard to impress.

Dylan explained that the song had some moments of Dolly Parton talking and I would speak those parts. He sang the verses.

As the song was happening, it was one of the moments when time seems to stand still. You know, like in a dream when you can't run away from whatever you need to get away from. That slow-motion weirdness continued on as we performed the song. When Dylan plunked the last note on his piano, I glanced up and saw Dill's face twist up like he had bitten into a lemon. He may have even said "Eww," under his breath. Laura didn't say much. What was there to say?

I walked back to my seat, wishing for that moment when I could turn into vapor and evaporate into the carpet. I couldn't breathe. All I wanted to do was run from the room and never go back. I was embarrassed and humiliated, and felt even worse for Dylan, who was clearly talented and could've produced something so much better with someone else.

I sat there wanting to sink into the floor the rest of the session. When things wrapped up, everyone gathered into groups to go to Benny's house for a barbecue. Benny was in Cycle 20. He was a big guy with warm brown eyes and a welcoming nature. He lived out in The Bronx and was throwing the party for all of us in Cycle 21. I'm glad I went, but at the time I just wanted to go home.

Clay, being the brother from another mother that he seemed to be to me, hung back and walked with me. We stopped at his house first before making our way to the party. It was strange that I had never met him before. I felt as if I'd known Clay forever. People in the class would ask us if we applied together or if we'd met before?

After Clay gathered up his things, we made our way to the subway. We got off at the stop that Benny had put into the directions. Once we emerged from the train, the streets were deserted. It was so different than the hustle and bustle we had gotten used to in Manhattan.

Clay seemed to know which way to go, so we went in that direction, but it was wrong, so we turned around. After walking for about 15 minutes, we made it to Benny's neighborhood. I smelled something grilling and it reminded me of summer days in Wisconsin. I wished, for a brief moment, I was back home. Sitting on a beach somewhere, toes in the sand, and listening to the waves of the water, breathing in the fresh

Midwest air.

We swung around the corner and down an alley that led to the backyard of Benny's huge place. All of Cycle 21 was already there, along with Cycle 20 and many faces I hadn't seen before.

Some people in our cycle glanced up to see me and looked away, embarrassed for me. I went up to Benny and thanked him for having us, and he slapped a big meaty burger on a plate for me.

"There you go, girl," he said with a wide, warm smile. He told me drinks were inside.

I made my way into what seemed like a mansion after living in my studio for the last few weeks. The hall was narrow and winding, and there were several flights of steps. When I arrived at the top of the stairs and stepped into the kitchen, I was relieved to see Maria dancing to some music and making hors d'oeuvres. She greeted me with a huge hug and asked me how the day went.

I let out a sigh that felt like it lasted for years. She asked what happened and I told her.

"Oh, it probably wasn't as bad as you think," she said.

"Oh it was, trust me. And now I can hardly look at Dylan or anyone else in the cycle, for that matter," I said.

Maria hugged me again and told me that things would get better.

I loved her energy. She was nurturing and inviting, and I was so happy she was there to listen. She had already been through the first year and reassured me, again, that it was the hardest year of the program.

I thanked her and made my way back out to the barbecue. I tried to shake off the discomfort I felt due to my overwhelming feeling of failure. Benny had invited people from other cycles and I found myself talking to them with a sense of ease. Perhaps it was the idea that they hadn't seen or heard the bomb I dropped earlier that day. Eventually, I was able to enjoy the party and relax.

As it got dark and the party started to disassemble, Clay and I made our way back to the subway. I'd forgotten how young he was until I observed how drunk he was. It was entertaining to watch him spin around the subway pole in the middle of the car, singing a song he made up called "Everybody Poops" at the top of his lungs.

After I arrived home, I flopped down on my hunter green futon and laid there, staring at the ceiling. Once again, I listened to my heart beat. My heart - that was so in love with New York for my entire life. I fought back a tear as I wondered if I belonged there at all.

My head said, *Your skin isn't thick enough, you're not talented enough, you'll never be a New Yorker, what were you thinking? Blah, blah, blah...*

Then I listened to my heart again. *You're all right and you're right where you're supposed to be.* With that I drifted off to sleep, waking the next morning still in my clothes, feeling as if I had just slept for 100 years.

I sat up on the futon and stretched out like a cat. The sun was beating into the apartment and I was starting to feel like I fried egg. It was time to head to class. Like a turtle, I wanted to stay at home and hide in my shell, but I knew there was no turning back, so I mustered up the strength to go.

 Dorothy Never Got Down Like This

"Lead with your heart today, not your head," I told myself. After all, it was my heart that got me there. Had I listened to my head, I would've done the practical thing, considered how much NYU was going to cost, and then continued eating cheese by the brick while binge watching *The Golden Girls*. No, this was it and I wasn't going to 'throw away my shot.'

I threw together an outfit I loved but hadn't been brave enough to wear and fearlessly went back out into Manhattan.

We were no longer in the Dean's office. We were now in what would be our Tisch home for the next two years. Though our class was the biggest the Graduate Musical Theatre Writing program had seen to date (32 of us), we were still a relatively small group in comparison to a lot of the other programs at NYU. Our thirty-plus group was given a floor in the Broadway building.

When I stepped off the elevator, I stepped into the student lounge. It was painted a sort of sky blue. Beyond that were glass windows looking into the office, and next to it was a classroom that overlooked Broadway. To the right of that were massive, heavy doors which lead into our black box space, which was where we ended up spending most of our time. Down the hall were practice rooms. That was about it, but more than enough for what we needed, although practice rooms were always booked to the gills. I took in our space, along with a deep breath, and reminded myself of the mantra I had said when I left the apartment earlier.

I heard the elevator ding behind me and Tres stepped off. He was on his phone as per usual and looked up.

"Hey Banana face, we get our first assignment today." Tres had a knack for knowing things before anyone else did.

I was never sure how he achieved this, or if I was just oblivious to things - which was probably the case. I followed him into the classroom and kept my head up, also telling myself that soon that train wreck of a lyric I wrote would be a distant memory. Tres and I plunked our weighty backpacks down on the floor and took the remaining two seats.

The professors followed, holding what we would soon discover was our prompt. But first, they would have to pair us up yet again. They called out the new duos. I was paired up with Ricky, a composer/lyricist who was a YouTube sensation of sorts and had been part of the dance company for Lin Manuel Miranda's first musical, *In the Heights*. Ricky was much younger than me, had a face like someone you'd see in a picture frame in a store and a beaming smile.

When we sat down to talk over our ideas, he took the time to share all the things he had done, which was great until he got to the part where he asked me what I had done. It sort of reminded me of the moment we first introduced ourselves and we all had to say where we received our Bachelor's degree. I was standing in a line that went something like this:

"I went to Princeton, I went to Yale, I went to Juilliard, I went to the University of Wisconsin-Green Bay (me)."

After I said the words, I did a little cheerleader kick punctuating how lame it sounded next to all of these ivy leaguers. I'm kidding - I didn't really do a cheerleader kick. Just in my head. Anyway, this was that same kind of thing - small town girl meeting New York up and comer. Before I let myself sink into the floor, I reminded myself of my mantra once again.

"Why don't we take a look at our photo prompt," I said,

taking the attention off of me and my nonexistent resume.

The picture we received was of a male stripper dancing for a group of women, all who appeared as if they were watching the sequel to *Magic Mike* and loving it, except for one woman in the back of the crowd.

Ricky and I gazed at the prompt, which seemed to beg for a humorous song. We chatted about a few ideas, but nothing jumped out at us. We left together, and between the elevator and the subway, I had, what I thought, was a stroke of genius.

"Hey," I said, "how about we write a song about the woman in the crowd making that face? You know, the one who looks like she's in the 9th circle of hell. We could call the song, 'It's Your Penis That Came between Us.'"

Ricky chuckled, and we chatted over some thoughts of what the story of the song could be. I was very pleased with the idea, thinking that leaning on my sense of humor might be my best plan after my first bomb with the Dolly Parton song. I could only hope.

I wrote the lyric and passed it off to Ricky, feeling good about it.

He came up with some fun, pop music and we had the comedian of our class, Betty, who was this adorable little blond woman with a raw sense of humor, sing it. She was hilarious, and we thought she'd be the perfect person to give voice to our song.

So here we were, the entire cycle huddled together in that same classroom where we received the prompt, the room with all the windows which faced Broadway. The rush of the city could be heard outside. My fellow classmates were shifting in their chairs as we waited to see who had to go first. The stakes seemed higher than the last exercise because this was our first actual assignment.

The faculty called out Ricky's name and my name as the first team to present.

Ricky glided over to take his seat at the piano and Betty made her way up to the front of the room. She was smiling, I was smiling, and Ricky was beaming as he placed his music on the piano. We were all sure we had a winner. The song started, and I waited for the laughter.

And waited. And waited.

The laughter never came. You could hear a pin drop. The look on Betty's face was one of surprise as she sang the last note with a crackle in her voice. The three of us had laughed over the idea, but apparently nobody else found it as funny as we did. She picked up her music swiftly and went back to her chair.

That high I had felt before the song started deflated like a helium balloon days after a birthday party. I sat still for a moment, dreading the next step of the process. The critique.

I saw Ricky pull a stool into the middle of the room for himself as I slogged my way over to sit next to him. If I could have chosen a super human ability at that moment, it would've been to turn invisible. There was nothing worse than that walk of shame to the stool after dropping another lyrical bomb on the ears of Cycle 21. I took the hot seat and -

Silence.

Is this really happening to me again? Where's the nearest exit?

Silence can be deafening when it's clear that your joke didn't land.

We sat there waiting. I felt like I was floating up to the ceiling - I think my brain was abandoning the situation at all costs.

Finally, David, one of the faculty members who had a knack for softening a situation, spoke. "Okay, do you guys want to tell us about your idea?"

That helped break the tension.

Ricky came up with something fabulous to say regarding his process that seemed to save him from the creative drought I was stuck in. When he was finished, I felt all eyes fall on me. Like a frog on a lab table, I was hoping for the first incision to be quick, but the silence continued to cut to the bone. I tried to be as clever as Ricky, but my words came out in unintelligible syllables - much like my lyric apparently.

Thinking back, I truly don't remember what I said. Not only did I feel like I failed again, I thought I failed my partner... again. I checked in with my heart one more time.

Um hello, you said I was right where I was supposed to be. Why did my song flop again? My heart didn't have an answer.

Chapter Twelve

Cheers to Dorothy -
Now someone help me get home

After writing a dick joke that fell flat, I decided to tuck away my middle school sense of humor and become the queen of ballads. Sadly, they were also really bad ballads. So, the next assignment went much the same as the first, and so on and so forth. I'm pretty sure everyone, including myself was wondering why I had been accepted into the program.

Beyond that, I wasn't intermingling with anyone. I'd get done with class, go home, and drown myself in a bottle of cheap Cabernet. I think one of the professors - Frank - noticed, and in an effort to get me out in the land of the living, he *assigned* Benny to invite me to outings.

I went out one night with Benny, Frank, Maria, and Nikki - another woman in Cycle 20. We went to a bar in Greenwich Village. It was another one of those funky places with low lighting and jazz music that took me back to what speakeasies must have been like. My only hope was to see a quartet of horn players jamming in the corner, but no such luck.

It wasn't long after we were there that someone decided we should have a round of Tequila. I'm a wino through and through, but with the pathetic prose cloud still looming over me, I thought a little Agave Nectar could only help my lame-ass lyrics. I did one shot, then another. Wow, it was really going down well. A few minutes after the final shot, I noticed my words were sounding mushy and the walls appeared to be sliding into the floor, which was a bummer, because I really had to pee.

I stepped down from the bar stool and slid my foot forward, as if I were walking on an ice skating rink with no skates.

I got this. I concentrated on my footing. I continued to slide my feet across the floor, knowing that if I lifted one I might topple over. I was keeping myself up well, or so I thought. Now, there was the challenge of finding the bathroom - in New York, the bathrooms are usually downstairs, across the street, or in the nondescript building with no signage that may or may not be owned by the mob.

I finally saw an open archway. I slid myself over there and saw stairs - of course. Sober that would've been fine, but after five or so shots of tequila and two glasses of wine, it felt a little more like climbing down rocky terrain in a blizzard. I gripped the railing and made my way down the stairs to the darkness below. When I reached the landing, I looked about to see doors in every direction. I opened the first one - a closet. Then the second door - the kitchen. *Really?* Then the third door - another closet? Okay, is this just to mess with drunk people?

I turned and saw the men's bathroom - I'm on the right track, right? Sure, except, no more doors. I crossed my legs and did a little dance, looking up at that flight of stairs, knowing there was no way I was going to get my drunk ass back up them without peeing in my pants. I looked back at the men's bathroom door, took a deep breath, and pushed it open.

Luckily, it was a one-person bathroom, and nobody was

in it, so I locked the door behind me and turned to use the toilet. Except there wasn't one. *WHAT?*

Resting on the bathroom wall was a urinal that seemed to be staring at me with a smile. I stood still for a second, scratched my head, and wondered just what guys did when they had to go number two. Before I could finish that thought (thank God), I pulled down my pants, put my back to the urinal, and stood on my tip-toes, trying to get my vagina somewhere in the vicinity of that porcelain perch without actually touching it with any part of my body, all the while trying not to tip over. It was at that moment that I realized I had too much to drink.

Somehow I peed, pulled up my pants, and made my way up the stairs in what seemed like a lot less time than it took to find the loo. Frank was dancing near the bar with Benny, Maria, and Nikki when I jumped up behind him and yelled into his ear that I had just peed in a urinal. News I'm sure he wanted to hear.

I tried to dance with the group, but it was more of an allover body dry heave, to which I saw Frank whisper something to Nikki. She made her way over to me and offered to take the subway home.

"But why?" I asked. "We're having so much fun."

We stepped out of the bar and I squinted, blinded by the bright lights of the city. My contacts were dry and foggy, and I could barely see a thing. As promised, Nikki stayed on the subway with me until my stop.

"You sure you can make it home all right?" she asked.

"I got this. Sure," I mumbled, and stepped off the train. I concentrated on my stride and watched as my wobbly legs

Dorothy Never Got Down Like This

swerved all the way to 74th and 1st. After taking about 10 minutes to get my key in the door, I stumbled in and peered up at the 80 steps I had to climb to get to my apartment.

"Well," I said aloud, "you'll be sober by the time you get to the top."

* * *

Even after my drunken extravaganza, Maria and Benny still wanted to hang out with me. A few weeks later, Benny invited me to his house for another party. I was all kinds of pumped, thinking that he might be interested in me. I watched as Mayasu had paired up with the lovely Ruth, and other people were finding mates or flings. The only companionship I'd found was tequila and a door-sitter, Warren.

Maria and I stopped at Trader Joe's and bought 2-buck Chuck, the lovely cheap bottled wine before taking the train out to Benny's. When we arrived, I walked in, handed Benny the wine, and noticed they had hung a hammock in the back of their flat near a window.

"Oh wow, a hammock!" I said.

Benny warned me to be careful as I ran up to it, but I wasn't. No sooner did I flop down onto it did the hammock flip me off (literally). I landed face first on the floor.

Benny ran over to me, asking if I was okay.

"I think so. Do I still have all my teeth?" I joked.

I dusted myself off and went to the dining table, shaking off my embarrassment. They dealt me in for a round of cards. We had such a great time, all the while, me making sad attempts at flirtation with Benny, as I was positive we were about to become an item. That was until there was a tiny knock at the door. I saw Benny smile his big, beaming smile.

"Come on in girl!" he said.

And in came a tiny waif of a woman. She flipped her hair back, threw off her coat, and came right over to the table and jumped into Benny's lap.

"Erin, this is my girlfriend, Bonita," Benny said.

God, I'm an idiot!

I kept a smile on my face until the card game was done, then I made it home to my place. There, I sat down on my trusty green futon and wondered how I got those signals wrong? Or maybe there weren't any signals. Maybe he was just being nice. Such was my life with men. I misread things a lot. I can't begin to describe the number of failed relationships I've had. They've all been humorous stories of failed first dates. Hmmm, problems with collaboration - do you see a pattern here?

Manhattan was lonely. I don't think I was even so much interested in Benny as much as I longed for a plus-one to hang with. It seemed so easy for some people.

I went out with Ruth and Mayasu one night and watched as they connected (and wondered what I was doing there, besides performing my act as a third-wheel). I laughed, thinking that my Scarecrow really was Clay - and thank God for him. He made me laugh and I found comfort in him like I would a homemade quilt. Upon that realization, I checked in with my heart again, knowing it would be okay. I couldn't dwell on it. I wasn't at Tisch to find a boyfriend. I was there to become a better writer.

It was the middle of fall and Thanksgiving was getting close. Clay was flying back to Illinois. I didn't have enough money to fly to Wisconsin twice (at Thanksgiving and Christmas) but I had an opportunity to visit Cade and his family in Lancaster. I was so grateful to him for asking me to come.

At Penn station, I bought my train ticket from the self-help kiosk and waited outside the gate to board. It never occurred to me that I had this innate sense of direction while living in New York. (Clay would probably disagree with me, reminding me of how many times I got lost.) I always felt like I could find my way and I was never nervous about it, thank God. I felt safe - like the city was a best friend who I knew so well.

I boarded the train and watched as the city slowly faded into the distance. The calm fields and valleys of Pennsylvania came forth and I felt myself relax in a way I hadn't been able to in months. I'd spent so much time trying to hold it all together - all of my raw emotions - that I didn't realize how exhausted I was.

I nodded off for what seemed like a second, only to be awakened by the announcer speaking under the muffle of an old P A system, "Next stop, Lancaster."

I gathered my things and waited near the train car door. It opened, and I felt like I was jumping out into the middle of nowhere. Picture that scene where Carey Grant gets off the bus in *North by Northwest.*

I took a moment to get my bearings and saw the train station. As I entered, I was in awe at the charm of the historical building. I went down the flight of steps staring at the ceiling, admiring the architecture. That's when I heard my phone beep. It was Cade.

I found him waiting outside with his two little ones, Woody and Lily. They were both mini versions of Cade. Woody, especially. He was very analytical, a nine-year-old going on forty-nine.

The kids had never met me before but greeted me as if they knew me. I gave Cade a huge hug, not wanting to let go of my friend. It was so comforting to see a familiar face, and one that I trusted and loved as much as him.

That Thanksgiving I was truly thankful to have that time with Cade and his family to relax. I lied in the bed in Lily's bedroom - they had fixed it up as a guest bedroom and Lily was temporarily moved into Woody's room - and let the last 5 months wash over me, wondering how the hell I'd done this.

I thought about how much it was costing me to be in New York. It felt selfish, to be spending all this money on something I might never be able to pay back. I wondered if I should just throw in the proverbial towel and go back to Wisconsin at Christmas and stay.

I remembered watching my mom stand in the driveway after she gave me a portion of her savings, so I could rent an apartment. As I had pulled away in grandmother's car, I saw her face. She believed in me. *What if I let her down?*

The next day, Cade, his wife Rita, Woody, Lily, and I went to the indoor Farmer's market in Lancaster. There was an undeniable charm about the quaint little city. We spent most of the day tasting cheeses (yay cheese!), maple syrups, and anything else that the vendors had put out to try. I envied Cade's life. I only hoped one day I would find myself settled somewhere with someone I loved.

Before I left Manhattan, my silver cross necklace had fallen into the drain in my bathroom sink, which didn't contain a stopper. I heard the necklace sail to a place I couldn't reach unless I took off the u-pipe. Since I didn't have a wrench (and had no idea how to remove a u-pipe anyway) there was nothing I could do, so I let it go for the moment. I liked wearing a cross - it reminded me that God was with me wherever I went. So, crazy as it sounds, when I noticed my train back to New York was the 666 train, I told Cade I had to go shopping to find another necklace.

Cade and Rita were busy that day, so they let me use their other vehicle to go to the mall in Lancaster. I stopped in a salon and got my haircut, window-shopped, ate a big pretzel in the food court, and found another necklace on sale with a pretty cross. It shimmered in the light (and would be the thing that would attract the man I was about to fall in love with).

The next morning, I said good-bye to Cade and his family and got on the 666 train. As the train rolled into Manhattan safely, I realized it had been silly to think something would go wrong.

I made it to my apartment, happy to see there were no roaches waiting for me - at least that I could see - and unpacked, preparing to head to Tisch the next day.

Thanksgiving break had been a welcome respite for me. Back at Tisch, we were given our next assignment, which was to watch three preselected films, discuss them with our collaborator, and write an extended sequence (of which none of us knew what that was) inspired by one of the films we chose.

We were nearing the end of the first semester and by that point, I felt I hadn't written anything substantial. I wondered if

I was even capable of composing decent lyrics. I also wondered if I would even have a collaborator to work with for year two if I stayed, since the second year was devoted to writing a musical with another student. I had pretty much decided I would tell my family I was quitting school at Christmas time and find a job in Wisconsin. I hated the plan, but I didn't know what else I could do.

For the film assignment, I was paired up with Soyhun Kim. She was one of the three females in our cycle from Seoul, South Korea. She was an incredibly talented pianist, able to play anything with a single peek at the music. She was petite in stature with an inviting personality and had the most fabulous collection of shoes I'd ever seen.

I was excited when we were paired up. I had a good feeling about her - she had always been kind to everyone without a trace of judgment. I could feel comfortable writing with her and not be afraid of a failure.

We decided to write our extended sequence for the film, *The Curse of the Golden Flower*. It was a Chinese film, and Soyhun and I decided we could use an Asian-inspired sound for the music.

We liked that the film featured a strong woman playing an empress who realizes her husband, the emperor, is poisoning her tea. (Spoiler alert) In the film, she dies, but Soyhun and I changed the ending in our extended sequence, having the empress kill the emperor with a hairpin in a badass *Kill Bill* sort of way.

And an amazing thing happened. As I went to write the lyrics for our piece, I realized I wasn't straining myself. I didn't feel like I wanted to pull my hair out or that I was bleeding out of my eyes. I felt *relaxed.* Finally, an actual lyric came out.

It wasn't perfect, but it was a hell of a lot better than anything I had produced before. Soyhun, being as brilliant as she is, asked one of her friends to play the haegeum - a traditional Korean string instrument. Adding that instrument gave the piece the haunting sound we were searching for.

I introduced the song in class. It was interesting what happened as soon as the first few notes of the haegeum were played. Everyone was suddenly struck by the unique and haunting sound of the instrument. Then, I watched as I finally felt what I'd been longing for - that feeling of satisfaction. Our song was successful. I spent some time enjoying the way that felt.

It was nearing Christmas. My flight to Wisconsin was in a few days and I had to make a decision. I was fairly certain I'd leave the program.

That night on my way out of the building, I passed David's office. I saw him sitting in there reading and felt an overwhelming urge to knock on his door. He wasn't my advisor that year, but he was easy to talk to. I thought perhaps, he'd have some parting words of wisdom for me.

He opened his door and a feeling of calm washed over me. He gestured for me to come in and I took a seat. He complimented me on my work with Soyhun and that made me smile.

Up until that point I hadn't heard much in positive comments about my pieces. I thanked him for his support and told him I'd be leaving the program at the end of the semester.

David seemed rather shocked by this, which in turn

shocked me. I'd been under the impression that everyone was thinking the same thing about me - that I'd quit. He went on to tell me that often, for someone like myself, who has playwriting experience, but not a lot of song writing experience, it takes a while for them to get warmed up.

"Erin, did you see how your work improved when you wrote a longer piece? You'll probably blossom next semester when you're writing the 10 to 20-minute musicals. You'll be writing an entire story, not just one song."

As I listened to David, a light bulb went on in my head. Suddenly, it made so much sense. I was used to writing plays. This intrigued me. Now all I wanted to do was stay, if only to see if it was true or not. I still worried if I would have someone to work with in the following year after having such a pathetic start. So I asked David's opinion.

He laughed. "Don't be silly, Erin. You still have half of the composers to work with yet. Don't worry. To be honest, it's very rare when the faculty doesn't have someone to pair up with someone else."

Much relieved, I was glad I had made that stop in his office. Had I not, I probably would've left NYU and never finished the program. David saved me from myself that day, and as I flew back to the Dairy State, I don't think I ever felt so proud of myself as I did then. Surprisingly, I was looking forward to going home, but I was also looking forward to going back over the rainbow after Christmas.

Chapter Thirteen

Dorothy got a Makeover

I returned home to Wisconsin and felt as if I was Alice after she drank the potion that made her grow tall in Wonderland. I felt like a giant! Like when you move out of your parents' house and then go back to visit your old bedroom. Suddenly what once fit you perfectly now seems too small. A friend of mine put it like this, "You're a Hermit crab and once you lose that old shell, you can't crawl back into it anymore because another one is coming, one that fits just right."

I spent a lot of time with family, but I could tell I had changed. My older brother was right. I was stepping into the person I was supposed to be, and much like Dorothy, I had to leave home to do it.

I allowed myself to relax during the holidays. I ate copious amounts of dairy and sat watching episode after episode of a TV show with Mom. I had time to unwind. Something I hadn't done much of since I started school. It was also a time to let everything that had happened sink in - I was no longer ignoring my dream. Now I was chasing it, and while I wanted to stop and let myself enjoy the holiday break, I knew I couldn't get too comfortable - it would only make going back to the Big Apple harder.

I did find myself getting cranky when it was time to leave for New York in January. Not because I didn't want to go, but that fear was settling in again. I didn't want to go back and fail. I had a feeling, however, that this semester would be much better than the first.

I landed in the Big Apple at the end of January, got a cab, and made my way to my apartment without batting an eyelash. A lot had changed for me from being that terrified girl who had landed there six months previously.

Clay called me while I was in the cab and invited me for dinner. I told him I had to drop my stuff off at my place and I'd be on my way. Already, I was getting into the routine again.

And that semester was so much better than the first. I was finally tossing aside that scared, insecure girl and adopting a brand-new shell I was fitting into.

The collaborations with other students went much smoother for me. In late March, we were assigned to write our first 10-minute musical. My collaborator, Kelly, was someone I had been looking forward to writing with. He was a composer who understood how to write for drama.

The prompt we were given was to base our short musical on a nursery rhyme. We chose Jack and Jill and decided to write about a seventeen-year-old lovesick boy who is a painter and asks his girlfriend to marry him. While the girlfriend goes for it at first, she starts to hear her parents' voices in her head and rethinks things. How we got that from Jack and Jill, I'm not sure. Like a lot of adaptations, it was "loosely based" on that source material.

When I started writing, I heard the voices of these characters quite clearly, and although the first draft was abominably long, the rewrite was much easier to set to music. Kelly agreed.

When we presented it in class, I was stunned by the

reactions. Clay played our boyfriend character and he was hilarious. My classmates were laughing hysterically (in all the right places) and I knew David had been right. I could write. I just hadn't found my footing until I was writing longer pieces.

After all of our 10-minute musicals were presented, Sasha came up to me. We hadn't spent too much time getting to know each other in the first semester. Probably because she intimidated the hell out of me. Sasha was this natural beauty and funny fellow writer from East New York, but she was one of the kindest, most generous souls I'd get to know in the program.

She said, "Erin, do you know you wrote one of the best 10-minute pieces in the class?"

Stunned, I stared at her for a second. Her wide, bright smile reassured me of the sincerity of her comment. I thanked her and let it sink in. Maybe Tisch hadn't made a mistake in accepting me after all. Maybe now I could finally get my head out of my butt…maybe.

That was our first 10-minute musical assignment.

The second ten-minute musical went equally as well. I was paired up with Basil. He was a relaxed and calm soul - a personality I found easy to collaborate with on the assignment. He seemed to trust me, as if he knew my ideas, though quirky, were workable for a story. He was easy to trust, and sexy - not that the two go together but it's a nice combination. Our writing prompt was to create a surprising moment that could happen at a birthday party or funeral.

After mulling over which idea we liked best, I blurted out, "What if we have a barber shop quartet show up at a funeral? That could be awkward."

Basil looked at me funny, probably with that thought in mind. Although he was skeptical, he asked, "Okay, what are they doing there?"

I went on to explain to him that the quartet could be honoring the dead. That the deceased had never told his wife that he was in a barbershop quartet, so the remaining trio shows up at the funeral to tell her. It is also revealed to her adult children the secret of how their parents met - in college, when they were both in an Acappella group.

One of the groups was called Chordiac-arrest, which got a big laugh during our presentation. And while Basil and I had set out to write a funny piece, it had an air of sweetness to it, with the quartet (minus one) singing to the wife of the deceased a song he had written for her before he died.

This assignment was probably one of my favorite pieces from that first year (not that there were a lot of good ones on my part to choose from). Basil was my first choice in terms of who I wanted to put on my list of collaborators for year two. I only hoped he would look past my earlier failures and put me somewhere on his list, too.

One afternoon sometime in late April we were all tired and trying not to nod off during a lecture (which the faculty seemed to understand because we were often up most of the night writing our assignments). I saw David walk in the room with a stack of papers. It was the list of who we were to be paired up with for our final assignments - the 20-minute musical.

Most of us knew who we were going to be paired up with because it was the person we hadn't worked with on any assignment yet. For me, that person was Clay. I wasn't sure

 Dorothy Never Got Down Like This

how we would work together as writing partners, but we were such close friends I could only imagine we'd at least laugh a lot during the process.

Our collaboration often involved me going to his apartment on the upper west side, lying on his bed while he played piano. He would sing ridiculous lyrics, like "everybody poops" or "my vagina's really lonely" which was him making fun of me and how unrelentingly single I was (my vagina was really lonely). I would laugh and add on to the lyrics, and he would yell at me to get off of his bed. I couldn't help it - it was so thick and plush. I never wanted to go home to my rock-hard futon.

Clay also had a way of being the occasional pompous ass. It took a while before I realized I could call him on it. Then he'd settle down and get over himself. I could've used a jolt of that confidence he had.

Our 20-minute musical was originally about a mentally ill homeless lady, but somehow, we veered off of that path and it ended up being a story about a young couple with a woman who was simply really afraid of commitment. *Hmm, who could that be about?*

The story changed entirely during the writing of it, which I found to be the most fascinating part of the creative process that I had to let happen. I equate it to carving a sculpture out of marble. You might have a general idea of the shape, but you won't know what the finished product will be until you step back and look at what you've created. It might not turn out the way you thought it would, but there is beauty in the process of watching it take shape and becoming what it is meant to become, or at least that was what I was discovering at Tisch.

We had an incredible director for our piece. NYU brought in amazing equity actors and directors for the students to meet and work with on their micro musicals. It was quite incredible watching these people read and sing our works. What an opportunity it was for us. To me, that covered the cost of admission right there (that, and maybe the organ or two I may have to sell to pay back my financial aid loans) but it was worth it.

We had a couple who was dating already perform our piece, which seemed to bring something extra to it - they already knew each other's idiosyncrasies.

After we finished our 20-minute pieces, we were ready to fly the coop, so to speak but I needed to breathe for a minute. I recalled what Jason had said to me about the first year at NYU when I met him in the bookstore. I now knew what he meant when he'd said, "It feels like boot camp."

And while boot camp was coming to an end, a new training ground was about to emerge. The great match game extravaganza in which we each made our lists regarding who we wanted to collaborate with in year two and the faculty paired us up.

The last month of the semester was the oddest in terms of the energy between everyone, which sort of felt a little like 8th grade before a middle school dance. We were all meeting with each other individually, trying to vie for that number one spot on the list of a person who was our number one choice. This process felt a little like online dating to me. I met with Basil, who seemed pretty positive, and while I thought I'd probably end up in his top 5, I knew I wouldn't be his number one (if you both put each other down as each other's number one choice, the faculty has been said to match you up). Then I approached Kelly and he seemed pretty non-committal. I also met with Ruth, who I really wanted to work with, but I knew she would be number one on many lyricists' lists. Finally, after all these meetings, we turned in our lists and it was left to hug expertise of the faculty.

It was tradition for the first-year students to go to a bar on St. Mark's Street - the same bar we went to the first night we all met - and wait for the results from the faculty. We gathered together and headed to the bar. The nervous energy followed us into the pub as everyone seemed to be sort of nursing their drinks and waiting patiently. I overheard bits and pieces of conversations. Betty asked me who I hoped to work with, and when I told her Basil, I noticed she was awfully quiet. The two of them had grown quite close and I realized she was probably his number one.

As I looked around the bar, I noticed everyone was sort of having little tete-a-tetes with each other. I took a deep breath and stepped outside, only to find a small group of my fellow classmates who all seemed to be joined at the hip. Envious, I stood on the outskirts of the group, realizing my lack of confidence over the first year had put me there. I had never imagined that at thirty-nine-years-old I would want to be part of a clique, but at that moment, I really longed to stand in their circle.

I had done it to myself, really, so I had to be realistic. They had all connected with each other on who they wanted to work with.

Trying to shake off my green-eyed monster while standing outside the bar in the brisk night air, cell phones started to explode from the many phone calls from collaborator to collaborator. Members of our class started to scream and hug each other.

I saw Ruth hug Beth. Clearly, they were a team. As I suspected, Betty hugged Basil, and on and on.

I stood apart from the group, feeling like the lone wolf, the one random person they couldn't find a partner for.

Then Betty said, "Erin, I think you're with Soyhun."

An email had been sent out to all of us with the complete list. I scanned it quickly searching for my name. Erin Hunsader/Soyhun Kim. When I saw this, I felt all my fear and tension release, remembering that moment Soyhun and I presented our song in class with the Haegeum. It was the first time I truly felt like I belonged at Tisch and I knew she was the right partner for me.

I called her, and plugging one ear against the noise of the street, heard her answer.

"Collaborator?" she said with a giggle.

I knew God had blessed me with the right person. Now we were tasked to write a fabulous musical.

Chapter Fourteen

Getting into Oz, Out of the Blue

Being at Tisch the next day was weird. It was as if we had all left as single the night before and came back as married couples. Everyone was in the black box, sitting next to their collaborator. It looked like the line at a wedding chapel in Las Vegas. Most students seemed content or pleasantly surprised with their partners. There were a few bombs that were dropped, but not too many.

I wasn't sure how Soyhun felt about being paired with me because she hadn't said much. I'd learned that she isn't one to gush about her emotions - that was my role in the collaboration, as we'd find out later.

All throughout year one, the faculty had stressed to us that it wasn't most important how you felt about each other's work. What was most important was that you wanted to write and compose the same things, essentially meaning, similar ideas and sensibilities. Truly good advice.

Soyhun and I went to Dojo, an affordable restaurant with an eclectic menu down the street from NYU. We sat near a window with the sun beaming in on us. We asked each other the big question. "What story do we want to write?"

We discovered we both wanted to write about women. Once we knew that much, we sat there, tossing around ideas. Soyhun told me about her host mother who she had met when she lived in Norway. Her Norwegian name was Randi. She had been adopted by a Norwegian family from an orphanage in Korea when she was six years old.

Soyhun explained that Randi told her the story of how she hid in her room for a year because she couldn't communicate with her new parents. She didn't understand why she had been taken from her home in Korea. As Soyhun shared Randi's life story with me, I realized we were both sitting there, overwhelmed by emotion, tears streaming down our faces.

"This is the story we have to write," I said.

She peered up at me with her strong, tear-filled eyes and nodded, without saying a word.

The second year at Tisch was all about collaboration. I knew if I hadn't run home crying in the first year, I wasn't going to do it now. I had watched during the first year as blow-ups happened in the hallway between collaborators in their second year. I'd scuttle by, hoping that wouldn't be me the following year.

But, as in any relationship, blow-ups were inevitable. It was how the situation was handled when it happened. The faculty often joked that the collaborations were like marriages. "Make sure you want to be in a relationship with this person before you put them on your list," was the advice we'd often hear in the first year. I had every intention of making the working relationship with Soyhun compatible.

Once we were paired up as a team, we were then paired up with our faculty advising team. Soyhun and I were lucky enough to be placed with the advising team of our choice. There was no time wasted as they reminded us that we had to bring them our ideas; the original idea - which Soyhun and I already had, plus an adaptation idea. And, regardless of which one we would be working on for the majority of year two, we were required to have a song or two for each. Cause writing four songs is easy!

As we had done before, Soyhun and I wrote overnight in her apartment, trying to pull together four songs. She had written this incredible, lyrical melody for a song for our original idea. The main character's birth mother had given her a music box. This music played when the music box was opened. I listened to her melody over and over. Then the lyrics just came to me.

We felt good about that song. Our adaptation idea wasn't as strong as our original idea, so we had decided to develop a concept loosely based on Soyhun's favorite musical, *Man of La Mancha*.

Our idea followed the story of an elderly lady from Korea who wants to accomplish her dream of singing on Broadway, except she has a terminal type of cancer. The woman begins her singing career as a busker on the streets of New York and in the subways. Along the way, she meets a young man. He works as an escort and is in love with a woman he doesn't think he's good enough for. The old woman changes his life, and he changes hers.

Okay, well, we didn't get quite that far with that idea either. When we went to pitch both ideas to the faculty, they noted that we had a better handle on the original idea than either adaptation. We were thrilled by this, because that was the idea we both wanted to write anyway. Our collaboration was off to a good start.

* * *

That moment when the witch flies over Oz and writes

Surrender Dorothy in smoke in the sky is a nice way to sum up my first year at Tisch. I had to allow myself to surrender to the incredible process I had become a part of and stop fighting it.

Unfortunately, it took me the entire school year to embrace it. It wasn't until year 2 that I fully realized I was actually *at* Tisch. Much like Dorothy's journey was about collaboration, so was my second year in the program.

When you begin a collaboration with someone, especially one that has you together day and night every day for months, it really is like a marriage - the faculty was right. You try to show your best face…until you're tired, hungry, and cranky. It's then when the worst of you comes out. Or, perhaps I should say, the worst of me.

I remember the first day at Tisch when faculty warned us that we wouldn't sleep much while we were in the program. I chuckled to myself, thinking of course we'd sleep.

Nope.

I quickly learned in year two of the program that sleep was something of the past, that it happened in 5 to 10 minute intervals whenever I had a free moment, like on the subway. Not really the best place to sleep, but sometimes the body gives up at the most inappropriate times. It's then that the Sandman wins.

During Year 2, I got in the practice of standing on the subway on the way to school so I wouldn't miss my stop. One time, I was standing next to a woman and we were both nodding off. I asked her if whoever got off first, we could wake the other one up. New Yorkers were very helpful that way - they all know what it's like to be overworked and exhausted.

In my second year I moved to Queens, and Soyhun and I only lived two stops from each other. It saved a lot of time when the trains were running smoothly - which was usually never, so it just put us closer geographically.

Getting back to the move, before the end of my first year, I had received a rent increase letter 3 months before my lease was up. The rental company would be raising my rent from $1525 to $1650.

Infuriated, I shared this information with my downstairs neighbor who had lived in the building since the dawn of time.

Shocked, he had said, "Wow, really? I only pay $750 per month, but then again, my apartment is rent controlled. It has been for years."

Wow, how do I get that type of situation?

So, that summer I knew it was time to find a new apartment. Needless to say, I was not looking forward to it. I'd moved so much in my life that the thought of moving again, and in New York City, terrified me. (And you all know how well the first search for an apartment went.)

People had told me to find my favorite burrow and move there. For me, that was Astoria, Queens after visiting my friend Lee there on numerous occasions. To get there, I had to take the N train to the last stop. My favorite part about riding the subway was the moment the train would arrive at Queens Borough Plaza. It'd come out of the dark tunnel into the bright sunlight, or if at night, to all the lights of the city twinkling back at me.

My heart was connected to Queens in a different way than it was to Manhattan. While I loved Manhattan, I wanted to live in a quieter place with more of a neighborhood feel.

Clay knew I was stressed about finding an affordable place, and I wasn't going to call Jerusalem or Bob again after what I went through the first time. I wanted to find a place without the assistance (and cost) of a broker. So, one day in August, Clay met me at my place on 74th and 1st, and we headed to the subway.

He liked the Astoria neighborhood, too. He had visited a friend there often and she had taken Clay to a local restaurant near the subway. It had become one of his favorite places.

After he and I looked at an apartment together, we walked to that café he loved so much. The new apartment was perfect and was $200 less than what I was paying in Manhattan. And the doorknob didn't even fall off.

As we walked, the sun beating down on us, I observed my shadow along the sidewalk. *I look like a giant. A really happy giant.* I was thrilled knowing this was about to be my new neighborhood, even though I had no idea how I would scrape the money together to move my things or pay the security deposit.

As I admired the houses that lined the streets, I noticed the yards were adorned with rose bushes. These brilliant bushes were bursting forth with scarlet, coral, and pink-colored blooms that hung over and out of the fences we passed by. I let my fingertips graze the tips of one, feeling the pedal's velvety feel in between my fingertips. This wasn't something I'd found in Manhattan.

As we continued our leisurely stroll to the café, I remembered something. About a month earlier, I had been lying on my futon in the middle of my studio in Manhattan.

The sun had been beating on my body through the windows. I had kicked off the sheets and lay there nearly naked, day dreaming.

Out of the blue, I heard a voice in my head say *he's coming*.

Okay, so I'll admit it, I hesitated about putting this part in the book, but every good story (or at least most musicals) have a love story, perfect or not. Also, as crazy as it sounds, it's how my brain works. Whenever I hear these things, whatever I hear, it usually comes true. (Okay, who am I kidding, it always comes true, but again, it sounds crazy.) Whatever this thing is in me, intuition or whatever you want to call it, (my older brother would call it something you shouldn't tell other people about) I have used it for a gauge throughout most of my life.

So when I heard those words that day while lying on my futon, I was excited. Excited, because I knew I was about to meet someone who would be significant to my life. And thank God, because my first year was lonely. Not lonely like one-glass-of-Chardonnay lonely, but lonely like do-I-remember-what-a-penis-still-looks-like lonely. I was in one of the biggest cities in the country and still felt totally alone. I wouldn't call this new guy my Scarecrow - that was still most certainly Clay. No, this guy I was about to meet was more like the Lion - a Greek lion.

It was no surprise to me that when Clay and I sat down in that cafe, before I even saw this new man who was about to come into my life, I heard the words loud and clear in my head. *This man is going to be very important to you.*

The hair went up on the back of my neck and then he appeared in my line of vision. He was setting water glasses down on our table when my mouth actually fell open. I had an image of falling in love with a New York guy. A tall, dark, and handsome man of Italian descent who had lived in New York all his life. He'd have a big Italian family that would yell at each other half in English, half in Italian.

At first glance, I thought he was the best-looking man I'd ever seen. Not quite as tall as I normally went for, but that didn't matter. He had black hair shaved down to his scalp, chocolate brown eyes, and an amazing body.

He greeted Clay and me with his swarthy good looks and New York accent. At that moment everything below my waist turned to gelatin. I couldn't even look up at him. He put the water glasses down, told us someone would be right with us, and scurried off. I must have watched him long enough for Clay to notice.

"You should tap that," Clay said.

"No," I responded, but in my head, I was already there and wow, it was hotter in my head than outside.

I didn't know when I would see him again, but I was sure he was about to become my lover.

   Dorothy Never Got Down Like This

Chapter Fifteen

Moving Vans, Traffic, and Parking Tickets

There's a theory that Oz was set in green tones in the movie to represent money and capitalism. While I'd scraped enough money together to secure the apartment in Astoria, I wished I had an endless supply of the green stuff to hire movers - or at least a horse and carriage to drop me off in Queens. I had neither.

I did have Clay and Tres to help me move. Thank God for them, or I'd still be running up and down six flights of stairs.

We picked up the moving van on a Sunday morning in late July and did a quick game of Rock, Paper, Scissors to see who was going to drive. We were all terrified of navigating the streets of Manhattan. Taking a deep breath, I decided I'd drive since it was my move.

As was typical of New York in July, it was a hot, humid day. Tres was in a permanent state of pissed even though he was trying to remain calm. He had ridden in the back of the moving van and been jostled around. After we brought the last item downstairs, I swept the place with a broom. I looked around, feeling a bit nostalgic. I'd only lived there a year, but so much had happened. So many laughs and tears had been shed. I had seen my first roach there - ah, the memories.

Clay snapped me out of my trip down memory lane when he reminded me that I had yet to have sex in New York.

We headed downstairs together, and I said good-riddance

to the six flights of stairs. We passed Jonathan - my hot Italian Super.

I'll never forget the day I first met him. I had purchased an air conditioner during the first month I was living there because of the relentless heat. He came to my apartment to fix something and asked me who was installing the A/C for me.

"Who put this in for you, your husband?" he asked.

I shook my head.

"Alright, I put it in for you, okay?"

Silly me, I agreed, thinking he wanted to genuinely help me.

Jonathan hoisted the unit up into the window and screwed it in place with an electric drill. It took him all of 10 seconds. Then he turned to me and said, "There. Now you pay me $50."

I felt so stupid that I had fallen for that. I heard my Wisconsin girl voice and New York girl voice arguing in my head. The nice Wisconsin girl said, "Just pay him the money." My New York girl was saying, "You're not paying for that. Kick him in the balls and then throw him out of the apartment!"

I paid him, although I did try to finagle the fee. He wasn't budging.

When I had passed him on my way out for the final time, Jonathan gave me a wink and a nod.

I wasn't sure what that meant. Maybe it was a flirtation, but I'd like to think of it as a sort of *you're a New Yorker now* gesture. As I got to the moving van and was about to get in, I noticed a bright yellow slip of paper under the windshield wiper. It was a $50 ticket for parking too close to a fire hydrant.

Okay, maybe I wasn't a New Yorker just quite yet.

"No," I screamed. Well, that made it easier to leave the city and move to Queens.

We drove to the apartment with Clay navigating. I pulled up to my new neighborhood, seeing those rose bushes that welcomed me the first time. It didn't take long to unload the van, and then Clay had to go to work. I discovered Tres was not as good a navigator as Clay. Tres was texting his boyfriend when he could've been helping me watch the ramps. Next thing I know, I was headed toward the Lincoln tunnel. There was more traffic than earlier that day and I white-knuckled it the entire way there. After the incident, I had a new respect for cab drivers.

That night in my new place in Astoria, lying in bed, I felt relieved. Before I fell asleep, I let myself revisit that moment a few months earlier, telling me someone was about to come into my life. It had been two years since I'd had a relationship and my body was beginning to feel like a plugged-up dam. I was so sick of masturbating that I was ignoring my own advances. I thought about my swarthy, olive-skinned waiter. I knew where I was going for breakfast in the morning.

I woke feeling refreshed, as if it was a new beginning. I showered and put on my favorite cotton dress. It was black with white stripes, had a sweetheart neckline so it showed a little bit of cleavage, and was extremely comfortable. I grabbed my purse, telling myself I was going to church, but I knew what was really on my agenda.

I practically skipped down the street, I was so happy to be in this neighborhood. Side note about Astoria - it has the highest concentration of Greeks anywhere in the world next to

Greece. The men are beautiful, olive-skinned gods. I'd never been interested in anything Greek before, except maybe feta cheese. Hearing their language and feeling the testosterone all around me, I suddenly became aware of all things Greek.

I headed to the café where Clay and I had stopped a few weeks earlier, hoping to see my swarthy New York waiter. As I stepped inside, my eyes scanned the dining room. I didn't see him anywhere. Disappointed but still hungry, the hostess asked if I'd like to sit in back.

I agreed, not realizing "the back" was an enclosed porch with no air conditioning. It was 90 degrees and so humid, I was sweating sitting still. I was melting. *Would I ever see him again?*

I was perusing the menu when I felt someone's eyes on me, well, actually on my breasts. My girls always know when they're getting noticed.

"Nice cross," he said.

He was referring to my necklace. I looked up and saw him standing beside the table.

We met each other's gaze.

His eyes were stunning - deep brown and strong. They reminded me of my grandfather's eyes. The rest of him didn't remind me of my grandfather at all. He exuded this sexuality that made my entire body tingle - something I hadn't ever felt before.

I must've stared too long because he said, "Look at mine." He revealed a gold cross around his muscular neck that had been under his shirt. He held it out to me on the chain.

   Dorothy Never Got Down Like This

"Feel it," he said.

I did.

"It's heavy, right? It's been weighing me down my whole life."

I couldn't decide if he was flirting with me until I heard the old guy at the table behind me tell his wife, "Our waiter's flirting with that girl."

My uterus skipped a beat.

Then the waiter told me his name and that he was Greek. Okay, so not Italian but being Greek works, too. Then he tried to guess my nationality.

"Are you Greek? You look Greek?" Alexandros asked.

"Nope," I said.

"Italian?" he asked, his attempts making me smile.

"Not even close."

Then, realizing his section was quickly filling, he looked at the people who had just sat down. He appeared to be disappointed. He met my eyes again and told me he'd return in a moment with my breakfast.

I ate my eggs, went to church, and dreamed about having sex with Alexandros instead of praying. I figure sex is a form of love and prayer is love, so it's all under the same umbrella.

On Wednesday, I went to get some more of those fabulous eggs I had on Sunday. I walked into the café and sat down. From the corner of my eye, I saw Alexandros. He saw me, too, and practically ran to my table.

He's running over here? No guy has ever ran up to me before. I thought my body must have been emoting how long it had been since I had sex. I greeted him using his name.

"Wow, you remembered my name. That's pretty good." He smiled.

"Yes, but did you remember mine?" I asked, knowing he wouldn't have because I had told it to him before he had a mad rush of customers.

"Yea, it's like Heidi or something?"

"Not even close. I'm Erin."

"Oh yeah, Erin. Where are you from again?" he asked, losing points rather rapidly.

"Wisconsin."

"Oh, yeah, right. I've never been there but I hear it's nice."

As Alexandros was talking, the waiter who had served me the day before passed by and smiled.

"You know him?" Alexandros asked.

"No, ah, he waited on me yesterday," I answered, embarrassed. I'd been there every day since Sunday looking for him.

"You were here yesterday?" he asked. "Were you looking for me? You were looking for me, weren't you?" He smiled a cocky, self-assured grin.

"No, I wasn't," I said, lying. "I came for breakfast."

"So Erin from Wisconsin, are you getting to know the

neighborhood?"

I remembered he had told me he had grown up in Astoria.

"No. I need someone to show me around." I heard myself say that and couldn't believe it had come out of my mouth.

"I can do that."

I agreed, and he gave me his pen for me to write down my number.

I saw he was looking over his shoulder at the gentleman I knew to be the owner, so I carefully hid my number in the tip money and gave his pen back.

I got up to leave when he called out my name.

"Erin! I almost ran after you. You forgot this." He handed me the Styrofoam box with the contents of the sandwich I hadn't eaten because I felt like throwing up the entire time I was there.

I had once given out my number to a NYPD officer I met at the Saint Patrick's Day parade after telling him that the NYPD should have a dating website. He seemed to think it was funny. He took my number but never called. I went about my day and figured I would never hear from Alexandros again. I'd have to find a new restaurant to eat breakfast at and someone else to show me around the neighborhood.

That night, around seven o'clock, my phone rang.

"Hello?" I said.

"Erin, what's up?"

God, his accent made me giggle.

"You love the way I talk, don't you?" Alexandros asked.

"I do." I had dreamed of moving to New York and dating a misogynistic man who sounded like he was from one of the *Godfather* movies. I mean, come on, what woman doesn't want that?

Alexandros was unusual. Despite his accent and the stereotype that went with it, he was incredibly articulate, smart, and a good listener. He surprised me when he asked me about myself and didn't talk about himself the entire time. He seemed genuinely interested in knowing about the program I was in at Tisch, even though I had to chastise him for being a native New Yorker and never seeing a Broadway musical.

We talked on the phone for three hours that night and by the time the conversation had finished, we had agreed to see each other either Friday or Saturday. He was elusive about why he might not be able to see me on Friday, but I was twitterpaited - as Clay put it, so I didn't care.

Friday came. I went to visit Clay at school. He was working in the office.

I was dying to see Alexandros but figured he wouldn't call until Saturday. A few hours later, my phone buzzed. I ran out into the hall for privacy and called him back. He told me he was free that evening and he'd pick me up in Astoria around 7 PM. It was five o'clock.

I ran in by Clay and sputtered, I was so excited.

"Okay, Erin," Clay said, "take a deep breath. Have a drink before he picks you up."

"No way, cause then I'll have sex with him immediately."

"So?"

"Ugh, no. No, I'm not having sex with him tonight. Not on the first date."

Who was I kidding. I knew I'd have sex with him that night and shouldn't have cared. But still a wrestling match ensued between the angel and the devil on my shoulders.

I left wondering why it mattered and thought about dating rules on the walk to the subway. The ride home was interesting. The angel on my shoulder was doing everything in her power to keep me from thinking about this delicious man naked in my bed. The devil on my shoulder…well, those thoughts were X-rated.

Don't change your clothes when you get home. Or, if you do, wear bad underwear, you know the ones that go right up to below your breasts and have holes in them. You will never have sex with him then. This was my guardian angel's sad attempt to convince me not to allow his aggressive Greek cock into my polite Wisconsin Whoha.

As much as I wanted to take it slow and get to know this guy, my body was feeling like a space shuttle that wouldn't launch. I hadn't been touched by a man in so long I was beginning to feel as if something was seriously wrong with me. As much as I wanted to fight my sexual urges, I had a feeling my body was going to win the battle before the evening was over.

I got home but didn't change my clothes. I reapplied deodorant, perfume, and touched up my make-up. Then my phone beeped again.

He's here already. I secretly loved the fact that he seemed excited to be with me.

I assume you need more time? His text read.

No, come on up, I sent back.

I just told this guy to come into my apartment. Now what?

I opened the apartment door and saw Alexandros coming up the stairs. I thought he was cute already, but when I saw him on the staircase I was stunned.

He looked up at me with his deep brown eyes and thick, dark brows and I melted like cheese on a basket of waffle fries. My legs gave out underneath me. I leaned against the door, trying to look like I had it all together.

He leaned in and kissed my cheek. Sweet, gentle.

I wanted to tear his clothes off. Aggressive. Dirty.

"Hey, I brought you a Greek frappe. I want you to try it. They're so good." He held it up for me to drink. It was nearly empty.

This was good. It took me out of my fantasy for a moment. I took a sip. "Mmm, this is good."

I gave him a quick tour of the apartment and then I checked something on my computer, leaning over the counter.

I felt his eyes on me. Again, more X-rated thoughts were running through my head.

"Damn, Erin, you've got a nice body." He sounded so sincere yet so surprised.

"Thanks. I've been working very hard at it this summer. I take boxing."

"Boxing? Really. Well, don't hit me," he joked. "You know I was born right around here."

"You were? We should go so you can show me where you were born."

"Okay, sure."

Whew, we made it safely out of the apartment. For a minute I thought I was going to be part of a Showtime original movie. *Wisconsin Girl Meets Greek God in Bed.*

We stepped out to the curb and he opened the door of his uncle's minivan for me.

His driving can only be compared to riding the Tilt-a-whirl at the fair. It was terrifying! The way New Yorkers drive in movies is nothing compared to the real thing. Alexandros was leaning over the steering wheel, his fist placed over the horn ready to honk at any second. He swore at people in Greek and Italian, stomping on the accelerator, then slamming on the brakes. I began to feel like a bobble head doll.

He drove around in circles until finally we were in front of a quaint brick house under the train bridge.

"I was born there," he said, pointing to the house.

"I can imagine what you were like as a baby," I said.

"My mom says I was like a box of matches."

From what I knew of him, I'd have to agree with his mother. He seemed explosive but in one of those this-is-not-the-kind-of-guy-a-girl-brings-home-to-meet-the-parents-but-he-thinks-he-is kind of way.

We drove around the neighborhood with me holding on to the doorframe and hitting the imaginary brake on the passenger side. He took me past the house where his yaya or grandma used to live.

"I miss Yaya," he said.

He told me about his family and how his father left his mother when Alexandros was in high school. He had become the man of the house, which was important in Greek families.

"You wanna go to the park?"

"Yes, please," I said, hoping for a relief from the whiplash.

We headed to Astoria Park, which was only a few minutes away.

He pulled over and parked near the curb. We got out and started down one of the paths toward the East River. I walked behind him for a moment and observed him. I liked his walk. It was powerful and confident. That was what I liked most about him - his confidence. He didn't care what anyone else thought, something I'd been working on for a long time. I wondered if that was what drew me to him and New York in general. There was a bravery and a confidence in both this man and this city that I wanted to achieve.

He was telling me about how much he liked the park when he leaned in close and took my hand. I felt fifteen again. We walked down to the water and looked across at the city.

"That's the Empire State Building," he said, gesturing toward it.

"It's beautiful," I said.

"So, Erin, do you miss Wisconsin, or do you want to stay here?"

"I do miss it sometimes, but I want to stay in New York."

He continued to ask me about what I liked about the city and how different it was from where I grew up. We sat on the cement ledge overlooking the water. He put his arm around me, and again, I felt that giggly schoolgirl bubble up inside me. I hadn't felt this way in a long time. I stretched my legs out in front of me.

"Ya' got nice legs, ya' know, like a dancer."

"Thank you," I said with a giggle. I loved his accent. I thought it was adorable.

"You love the way I talk, don't ya'?" he asked.

"Yes." I smiled.

Then he leaned forward, and I knew what was coming. I couldn't believe the butterflies tumbling in my stomach. It had been so long since I'd been kissed. Then it happened! His kiss was incredibly sensual, and kind of blew me away.

I had seen people kissing in the park and today I was one of those people. We kissed again and talked before we walked through the park again. We got to the other side, near his van.

My stomach wasn't ready to go back on the road with him just yet, so I planted myself on a nearby bench. It was nearly dark. The city was so pretty and peaceful from where we sat across the water.

I laid down on the bench, putting my feet across his lap. He rubbed my legs as we talked. I felt content in a way I hadn't in a long time. It became dark and we kissed until our lips were nearly chapped.

We stood up and started back toward the van. Was this really happening? Who was this guy? He was the Greek lion I was about to fall in love with.

Chapter Sixteen

Dorothy Never Got Down Like This

While I was in my undergrad studies, I tried to write for magazines for extra money. This was in the 1990s, before the internet existed. I researched all of the publications that paid contributing writers. An erotic well-known magazine for women was one of those magazines.

I went to a convenience store around 9 PM to purchase the magazine to research what kinds of articles they were looking for. When I asked the clerk behind the counter for the magazine, he stared up at me, licking his lips.

I asked for it again and he reached behind him. He pulled the magazine out of the slot without even flinching and slapped it on the counter. He leaned forward and whispered the price to me with a chuckle and continued to lick his lips - if he was trying to be sexy I hated to tell him it was more creepy than sexy.

I pulled cash out of my pocket, threw it on the counter and grabbed the magazine. It was covered in plastic, like its own personal condom. I snatched it up close to my chest and ran all the way out to my car.

I got home and peeled the plastic off of the magazine and read the articles. I was stunned.

Women were having fabulous sex! They were having two or three or EIGHT orgasms and writing about it. I, on the other hand, was not. I was in my early twenties then and I could've cared less about sex. If someone I was dating would have asked me to have sex or paint his bedroom I probably would've asked him what color we should use.

I couldn't write about fabulous sex unless I was having it. Finally, at thirty-eight years of age I had fabulous sex. But not because of Alexandros. He helped of course, but it was because of how I felt about myself.

Prior to this point in my life I had been doing things to please others. For the first time, I felt completely confident, comfortable, and beautiful. That night, while my angel and devil were wrestling, there was a point when I decided I was going to sleep with him.

He dug in his pocket for his keys. I could tell he thought he lost them. Then he said, "You know, we take on traits of the people we sleep with."

"Really, so what's going to happen to me?"

So that was out there now. He knew he had the green light.

We drove around for a few more hours, me hoping he wouldn't hit anyone with the van. He was entertaining though, I have to admit.

We stopped for wine, and I heard him speak Greek to the cashier. I could've listened to that all day, it didn't matter what he was saying. *It was an okay Chardonnay. Okay great, I'll take it, just keep speaking Greek to me, I mean…to the cashier.* The man showed us a nice Shiraz (I hate Chardonnay) and Alexandros purchased it.

We headed back to my apartment. As we stepped out of the minivan and onto the sidewalk that was the threshold of my home - my sanctuary - I knew if I let this guy in tonight then that would be it. I could call Clay and tell him to write a new song about my no-longer lonely vagina.

As we walked towards the steps, I realized it was my last chance to tell him that I wanted to go upstairs alone. The angel on my shoulder was pleading with me while the devil was taking off her panties.

We went in, had some wine, and talked for hours. He asked me what I wanted to write about. I told him I wanted to write television shows one day, but essentially, I wanted to write anything and everything. Little did the poor guy know I was going to write about him one day.

Our conversation went on and he stayed on his side of the room. He didn't try to kiss me once. He was a perfect gentleman. At about 1:30 AM he looked at his watch.

"Erin, I'm sorry, but I have to go. I have to get up early for work in the morning."

He headed down the hall to my bedroom to retrieve his phone that was plugged into my charger. It was at that moment I realized what he was doing.

I waited in the living room. He seemed to be taking an awfully long time. I called to him, but he didn't answer. I went down the hall.

He was standing there in the dark - super smart man.

"I'm just checking my email," he said.

Sure, whatever.

He sat down on the bed.

I sat down next to him and we chatted a bit more.

He leaned over and kissed me. His hand met the small of my back as he told me he wanted to kiss me some more. And so he did. He kissed my cheeks, my neck, my shoulders, all the while speaking Greek words in my ear.

OH MY GOD!

At this point, the only way for me not to have sex with this man would be to have taken a gun from under my mattress and shot myself. I pushed him back on the bed and was on top of him. I saw him smile in triumph. He'd seduced me, and I let him.

Sex with him was like having gelato after years of having vanilla ice cream. I mean, vanilla ice cream is pretty good, but gelato is SO much better. Well, maybe not better, but different. And he was different than anyone I'd ever been with. He told me what he wanted, and in turn, asked me what I wanted. What a concept - communicating during sex.

He was so passionate, caressing my legs, arms, and stomach all the while telling me what he liked about me. This was new for me, too. I'd never had anyone tell me *all* of the things they liked. He even said he loved how curvy I was. This won him lots of points.

Afterwards, we laid in bed talking. We fell asleep next to each other for a few hours.

He sat up abruptly and shook off his sleepiness, realizing he had to leave.

I knew he had to get up early for work. I put on my robe and helped him find his clothes in the dark. He kissed me in the kitchen and told me how fabulous I was before he left. I walked him to the door, kissed him again, and he was gone.

I wouldn't see him again for several days.

* * *

When I was a freshman in high school I fell in love with an older man. Up until that point I had been taller than most of the boys I went to school with and was usually teased for it. My older brother was a senior in high school that year and had a myriad of cute friends. The one I fell in love with was probably the one who was the least likely to ever be boyfriend material. He was tall with dark hair and grayish blue eyes. He was quick-witted and sarcastic, all of which I found immensely charming. He was the only person who could catch me off guard with his words. And, he seemed to take an interest in me, or so I thought.

His name was Rob Dillion and was the coolest guy walking as far as I was concerned. I was certain, as certain as Laura Ingalls Wilder was that Almanzo would be her husband, that Rob Dillion would be mine.

At first, he treated me like a sister. As I got to know him better over the next two years that he spent every day after school at our house, he became not just my brother's friend, but my friend. I'd run home after school to see him. Really, I was a dork.

There was even a time when I lost a bet and had to clean his car. It had so many fast food wrappers and soda cans in it that I wasn't sure how he was still alive. Rob taught me how to drive that day.

I almost put his car in the ditch, but it was a memorable moment.

At the end of my freshman year of high school he stopped over. It was the first day of June. He came into the house and sat next to me. He talked to me about random things, his eyes on the floor the entire time. He looked up at me, took my hand, pulled me towards him, and kissed me.

I still remember the moment because it was the first time everything around me stopped. The only thing I remember that kept going was the Steve Winwood song in the background. The video of "Higher Love" was playing on MTV.

He didn't look at me when he was done kissing me. He got up and left the room.

I sat with my head and lips frozen in a position as if I was prepared in case he'd come back to do it again. I thought something monumental had just happened, like it was a turning point in our relationship.

Until the next day when he called.

"Hey, is your bro there?" Rob asked.

"Yeah," I said. I let a long pause occur before I asked him a question. "So, what about…?"

"What about what, Erin?"

"Were you drunk last night?" I asked.

"No. Why?"

"Do you remember what happened?"

"Yeah," Rob said.

There was another long pause after he said *yeah*. He didn't have anything to say to me and I realized the kiss didn't mean anything to him. He was a senior in high school and was probably used to kissing many girls.

I was a freshman and that had been my first real kiss. This was a good lesson for me. Too bad I didn't remember it throughout the rest of my life.

So it was with the Greek.

Alexandros came over and stayed the night.

The next morning, I got up to brush my teeth. I came around the corner only to see him standing at the foot of my bed, dressing.

I went to the kitchen and he came out after me. He asked me if I wanted him to stay. I ran my fingers through my hair and sighed.

"I have to go get some coffee," he said.

He tried to be sweet, but I could sense he was ready to bolt.

I said good-bye to him at the door and hugged him tight. I thought about how safe I felt with him. I opened the door, watched him leave and assumed I would never see him again.

We texted back and forth for a few days, but the texts were different. It wasn't the fun banter anymore. He sounded a million miles away on a Greek island somewhere.

I headed to Midtown one day about a month later and popped into the diner for a muffin in a sad attempt to see my swarthy Greek waiter. I scanned the café for Alexandros, if only to see if he missed me.

I stood at the counter and felt his eyes on me. I looked up

and met his gaze, which sent a tingle through to my toes (that were crammed in very uncomfortable high heeled sandals).

"Erin, look at you. Wow. You look good, really good, and tall."

He always liked to note my height. It seemed to amuse him. "Are you headed to Midtown?"

I said yes, wondering how he knew that.

"Well, something's gonna happen for you soon," he continued. "You've got that shine about you."

Who was this man and why did he have to say incredibly intriguing things like that? *Bastard.*

I walked to the subway feeling a bit miffed and like my efforts were thwarted. He clearly had moved on. I kicked off my uncomfortable heels, wondering why I could never pick the right guy, or why he couldn't have been the right guy, and why the subway stunk like fish. I didn't have the answer to any of those questions and my feet hurt.

That was the last time I saw Alexandros for three months. We continued to text back and forth occasionally. I'd say we had become friends, at least via the phone.

When Hurricane Irene happened in August, 2011, I freaked. I'd never been in a natural disaster before, so naturally I reached out to him, knowing he was a native New Yorker. Sitting on my bed as the rain pelted the windows, I asked him what I should do.

"Tape your windows," he said in a very vapid voice.

I thanked him. *He was a good guy, just not mine.*

   Dorothy Never Got Down Like This

It wasn't until November that I saw him again. I was in the thick of things with Soyhun as we continued to crank out songs for our musical. I was proud of what it was turning out to be.

Alexandros got in touch to see how things were going, which led to a long string of texts and a lot of phone flirting. He asked if he could see me that night, and I assumed that meant we'd end up getting physical. While I wanted to accept that this was the only relationship I was going to have with this man, I knew I wanted more.

We agreed to meet at a pub near my house and have a drink. And, what I predicted would happen did.

He texted me the next day to see how I was. I think that was sweet of him. But, once again, I was upset. I wanted a relationship, not just the occasional fling.

Months went by and then, in March, he called me. I was sitting in my apartment writing when I saw his name light up on my phone. I debated answering it.

I picked up the phone and went into my bedroom.

"Hi," I said.

"Hey, it's the famous authoress. How are you?" Alexandros asked.

"I'm good."

"I thought you might be mad at me. You're not mad at me, are you?"

"Why would I be mad at you?" I asked.

"I don't know. You offered to make me dinner in your last text and then you canceled."

"I know, but that's just 'cause we can't be in the same room with each other without having sex."

Something in my gut told me his calls and texts came at a time after he'd been wounded by some other woman he was sleeping with.

He asked how I was.

I told him I was getting nervous about what was going to happen after graduation. I really wanted to stay in my apartment in Astoria.

"Why can't you?" he said. "Just put it in God's hands."

I said good-bye to him, but that question was still out there - just what was *I* going to do after graduation?

Chapter Seventeen

Out of the Blue Beginnings

Had Dorothy ever longed for Oz after she was back in Kansas? Maybe. I became this person who longed for Wisconsin when I was in New York, and vice versa. Eventually, I realized they were both home. I had to allow myself to be happy when I was in each place because eventually I would be back - either in the calm of Wisconsin or the chaos of New York.

The last semester of school I felt a bit like a squeezed lemon. The more I thought I couldn't write one more lyric or crank out one more song, the more I would be squeezed to meet a deadline. It's incredible to me, to think that we wrote a 90-minute musical in the span of eight months. And it wasn't something you just turned in and that was that. No. NYU brought in big Broadway performers and directors (much like they did at the end of year 1 for our 20-minute musical). The best part about that, besides watching these hugely talented people perform your work, was the feedback they gave us. It was invaluable.

Our musical, *Out of the Blue*, was scheduled for the last day of the semester, and, while I wanted so much to enjoy those final weeks of school, there just wasn't time. We watched as everyone who had already presented went off to enjoy the wonders of the city. We were still cramming to complete the end of the show. Soyhun and I laughed, noticing that it seemed like we had three different endings. But the story we had started with never wavered. While Soyhun and I noticed other collaborative teams were abandoning their ideas, our storyline seemed to be the one thing keeping us moving forward. It all started way back with that story Soyhun had mentioned at Dojo that was based on her host mother from Norway, Randi. The faculty, being ever so clever, mentioned that we should set it in Green Bay.

"Then your home is in the story, too, Erin," they said, which was helpful because it was so easy for me to write about Wisconsin.

After all of the late nights, compromises, rewriting songs in our sleep and minor meltdowns, we finally did it. The day of our final presentation I will never forget. Soyhun and I both agreed we wanted to write a story with a humorous tone, but we also wanted it to touch people's hearts. We never expected the reaction we got.

We were literally in rehearsal right up until it was time for our show. But finally, Soyhun and I took our seats in the packed black box at NYU and watched our story come to life before our eyes. Our lead actress (who is now a Tony winner) was pregnant at the time, which seemed so ironic and yet special to us, as she played our main character who starts the show waiting for the results of her pregnancy test (which comes back positive). She also had such a good grasp on the sarcasm and comic timing needed to play Jenny, who is a sixteen-year-old with a very snarky sense of humor. The show takes the audience through Jenny's journey as she tries to search for her birth mother, while trying to figure out what to do about her pregnancy. The story is about how she comes to realize that, in searching for her real mother, it was her adopted mother all along who took care of her and loved her.

As Soyhun and I soaked in every moment, we started to notice something amazing happen toward the end of the musical. While we had made people laugh throughout, we also saw that people were crying (in places where we hoped they'd cry.)

I looked over and saw tears streaming down Soyhun's face. I hugged her as tight as I could. We had worked so hard, I felt like she was my sister now. The show ended, and I wondered what would happen to it. Would the score sit on a shelf at NYU? I couldn't let myself think about that.

And so, I graduated. God knows I never thought I would see the day. My parents actually came. Meeting them at the airport was the strangest thing. I knew mom didn't travel well and my father hates cities, but when I saw them coming toward me in LaGuardia my jaw dropped. They were both dressed like they had stepped out of a picture frame. They looked calm and really together. *Who were these people?*

The next day we went to the graduation ceremony at Yankee Stadium. I'm not sure if Dad was more excited about me graduating or getting to go inside Yankee Stadium. It didn't matter - they were there. Afterwards, we went to Chelsea to have dinner with Soyhun and her parents. I had flagged down a cab near the stadium and we headed in that direction. I was sitting in the front seat of the cab, and glancing back at my father who looked a little rattled, I asked him how he was doing.

"I feel like Tony Soprano," he said, causing us all to chuckle. I glanced at my mom who was staring out the window with a look of satisfaction. I remembered that day in the driveway, seeing her face as I drove away, hoping I'd make her proud. I could see I didn't have to worry about that anymore. I was relieved she was proud, but I wasn't sure how I felt. I was pretty sure I was terrified of what was to come next.

When you're in a graduate program you're in a bubble. I felt like a fairy floating around in my secure little financial aid bubble. When graduation day came, that bubble popped.

I went back to Wisconsin for a brief time and got treated like royalty. Never mind that I was unemployed and clueless.

When I got back to New York in June, I walked into my apartment and found a big dead roach on the floor. (At least it was dead.) I started sobbing. I wanted to go back to Wisconsin and stay. Who was I to think I could ever make it here in the Big Apple? I was a cock-eyed optimist from the Midwest who was still waiting for my life to get better. I glanced around my apartment. Nothing was holding me there.

"Erin, this is it," I said aloud. "You've done what you had to do. Now you can leave."

Every time I thought that I could leave, New York, like an old friend, brought me something amazing. The summer before it was two scholarships I'd won.

I walked around that week looking for something to keep me there. Anything. Some sign, no matter how small, to give me a reason to stay.

I observed a mother bird ducking inside of a metal awning to feed her babies which I took as a sign of spring and new life - all that crap. Anyway, I took it as a sign to try to stay. And if I was going to do that, I'd have to find a job, and quick. The first of the month was near and rent was due.

At the end of the week, I headed out of my apartment to NYU. I had picked up some hours in the office to help supplement my non-existent income. I thought I saw something on the sidewalk ahead of me. I wasn't sure, so I got a little closer. It was one of the baby birds and it had fallen out of its nest. I walked away from the dead bird, grateful to be wearing sunglasses. I couldn't stop crying. It had looked so innocent lying there, fully formed, with its little beak partially open. It seemed metaphorical to me at that moment. I had been pushed out of the NYU nest and just what the fuck was I going to do now, except land with a splat on the pavement. I needed a job!

I'm a big believer in going with my gut. My gut told me quite clearly that the first job I took after graduation wasn't right for me. My gut said, "Hey, this job isn't right for you and if you take it, it can only end badly. Oh, and by the way, your gut would really like a corn dog."

Prior to graduation I had been looking for jobs, but nothing panned out. As the hours ticked by into days I knew I had to cough up rent for August. I had the foresight to pay June and July ahead of time and I was determined to stay in my place in Astoria - the giant occasional roach be damned.

I sent out a plethora of over-achieving resumes written in a ridiculous small font, with everything on it except a photo of my MFA.

Then crickets.

There wasn't one single, solitary response to any of the jobs I applied for. Not even a rejection email. Nothing.

I had found an advertisement on Playbill.com looking for a marketing and public relations assistant at a small theatre. It was in Midtown near Times Square. The job description was similar to what I had done at the Fox Cities Performing Arts Center in Appleton before graduate school, so I tweaked my resume a bit and sent it off.

Much to my surprise, the next morning I had a call from the manager of the theatre. They wanted to meet with me. Although she sounded lovely, she had that curt New York tone in her voice as she told me about the job and then we scheduled an interview.

Before I could spit out one syllable I was meeting with her later that day.

I assumed she either needed someone desperately or she was a horrible beast to work for, or both. I grabbed my best dress and uncomfortable heels and jumped on the N train for Midtown.

It was a warm, windy day but I loved it. I wanted to spin up the street in my dress. I was on my way to my first interview in Times Square.

I found the small door below the awning and stepped inside. All the joy in me jolted to an abrupt stop as the door swung shut behind me. It was the sort of feeling I had when I went to interview for a summer camp job that may not have really existed. Something in the energy in the room didn't feel right.

A man behind a ticket booth peered at me with squinty black eyes. He looked like he had come from the gym and wanted to lift me up and toss me across the room.

I smiled, saying I had an interview.

"Go sit in there," he mumbled.

I looked to where he pointed and started forward. This space was a little cheerier, with large windows and the sun beaming in - a rare thing to find in New York buildings.

I sat at a high table, peering out a window, wondering why I felt as if I wanted to jump out.

A petite, blonde woman dressed all in black with silver heels came out through a door that seemed to appear out of nowhere. She stepped toward me, her energy much different than the hulk at the door.

She shook my hand and we began chatting. She was relaxed and confident. I had a moment where I thought I wanted to be like her one day. She asked me several questions, all of which I felt I answered well. I was at ease and relaxed with her.

She asked me what I wanted to do now that I had graduated. I told her I wasn't sure, but said I wanted to find a job using my writing ability, which is why the job looked interesting. I would be writing copy, advertising shows for the theatre.

When we finished the interview, she offered me the job.

That's when the hair stood up on the back of my neck. While I thought it would be a good fit, something was telling me to think about it. I smiled and said, "Can I let you know tomorrow?"

"Oh, of course. In fact, why don't you come to the show tomorrow that you'd be promoting to see what you think."

With that, she told the big bulky guy to print me two comp tickets and she disappeared behind the invisible door again.

On the way home, I ran through the interview in my head, wondering why something that seemed to go so well made me feel so strange. I stepped off the N train at Ditmars and walked home, still lost in thought about whether or not to take the position.

"Looking for something?"

"Huh? Oh, hey Stevie," I said.

Stevie was a bartender at Fatty's on the corner of Ditmars and Crescent. I had gone in there one night when I first moved to the neighborhood and we discovered we were both musical theatre writers. We had a lot in common. He had quickly become a good friend. When he saw me, he noticed I was lost in thought.

"What's up, Erin? You look perplexed."

"I just came from an interview. It was so weird." I told him what happened. He agreed it all sounded positive until I told him where the interview was. He nearly spat his latte out onto the sidewalk.

"Oh shit, Erin - you had an interview there?" he asked.

"Yeah. What's wrong?"

"That's mafia!"

I nearly choked on my mocha. "What?"

"Yeah, how do you think that theatre stays in business. Have you seen the show?"

"No. I'm seeing it tomorrow."

"Oh." Stevie laughed. "Well, just wait until you see it. You'll see what I mean."

"If it's mafia I can't work there."

"Why not? You could write about it."

"Yeah," I said, "or I could get killed."

"No. They don't kill people anymore, I don't think."

I wasn't sure what bothered me more about that sentence. The fact that I had an interview with people who may or may not kill people, or the fact that it was a question of whether or not they were still doing it. The only thing I understood was why I had such an eerie feeling when I walked in the door for the interview. It also explained the big bouncer guarding it.

I have an overactive imagination. When Stevie told me this, I stayed awake in bed all night thinking that if I said no to the woman regarding taking the job, they would come and leave a bloody theatre mask in my bed to get their point across (ala the horsehead from *The Godfather*). I'd at least go see the play since I was given comp tickets, but I was too afraid to go alone. I texted Clay, who immediately asked why I was texting him so late.

Are you having sex? he asked.

I wish. No. I need a plus one to go with me to this play tomorrow.

He agreed, and I was able to fall asleep.

I met Clay on the corner near the theatre the next afternoon before the matinée and shared with him everything Stevie had told me. He let out a sarcastic chortle.

"Oh, this will be fun."

When we stepped inside, we saw the big bouncer in the box office. He squinted at me and cracked his version of a smile. He grunted and told me to go through.

Clay and I stood in the lobby waiting for the doors of the theatre to open. There were a total of 6 people seeing the play besides us. We found our seats and sat waiting for the show to begin.

I was the eternal optimist. *How bad can it be?*

I had no idea. I don't want to rip apart any play because I know that any and all theatre takes a tremendous amount of effort by all involved. This was a train wreck that ran off the rails, turned a corner, and never came back. That train went through an imaginary door into never, never and why, oh why, land.

At intermission, we sat stunned in our seats. I sent Clay a text. It read: *What's happening?*

He returned my text with a text of his own that was just question marks.

We went out into the lobby to get a drink to help us get through the rest of the show when we overheard one of the other patrons say, "I don't think we got what we paid for."

You said it, sister.

I took a deep breath and we went back in for the second act, which unraveled in such a way that it was almost impressive how little sense it made.

The next day I held my breath and called the manager, declining the position.

Now here I was again, with no job and no prospects.

Clay and I were both on the hunt for gainful employment. It was late June and I knew I had to make rent for August.

I swore I would never ask my family for rent money and miraculously I had managed not to.

The job I snagged should've been perfect for me. The position was in sales, not really something I wanted to do, but it was a company in the theatre biz. I thought it would be a good fit. This was the job my gut said wouldn't be a good fit for me, but I needed a job, and it wasn't run by the mob, so I thought I might as well take it. So I did. The job made me realize how exceptional the training was that I received at the Fox Cities Performing Arts Center in Appleton before I moved. That was a small but well-run operation. This theatre company was a hot mess.

I went into work one Monday morning to see the files on my desk that I had neatly stacked on Friday strewn across the desktop. I turned to my boss and another co-worker. "Did someone need something from my desk?"

They looked at each other and smiled. I guess it was fun for them to trash a co-worker's desk. It wasn't long after that incident I started praying to get fired. After nine long months I did. The company wasn't doing well financially (or so they said) and I was the last hire, so the first to go. I was ready to move on, but to what?

Chapter Eighteen

Kicked Out of New York

Although I went into the bathroom and did a little happy dance when I got fired from the bizarre-o-world, I didn't think ahead to the fact that I was without a job. I told Clay who was also employed with the company and he was stunned.

As I headed out of the building, my heart sunk. I may have struggled to find my place there, but I had enjoyed my job.

I walked to the subway, staring at the street numbers on the tile. Suddenly it was clear, as if New York was saying, "I'll miss you if you go."

My lease was up at the end of May and it was March. I knew if I didn't have another job by April I'd have to leave. As the days passed, I wondered if this might be an opportunity for me to reevaluate my situation.

While unemployed, rather than spend all my brainpower trying to figure out how to afford anything, I bought a cheap plane ticket back to the Midwest for a visit. I hadn't been home in nearly a year. I needed an extended stay and time away from New York.

While in Sturgeon Bay, my friend, Mary let me know that she needed help at her performing arts school that summer. Knowing I didn't have a job and my lease was up soon, it sounded like a good option - or at least a temporary solution.

I still had a month to look for work in New York and if I

didn't find something, I had a plan B. I could move back to Wisconsin for the summer, if need be. Of course, my plan B meant leaving my apartment in Astoria.

Despite the gigantic water bug that would meander in now and again, I loved my place and the neighborhood. I was close to Astoria Park, I had friends in the neighborhood - it felt like home. How could I pick up and leave that now?

A month flew by and still no job possibilities opened up. I, sadly, gave my notice to my charming old Greek landlord. I spoke a little Greek to him (the little I knew from living in the neighborhood) and he said, "Oh, your pronunciation is so good. Perhaps you'll meet a nice Greek boy."

Yeah, whatever. Been there, done that. And just where was the Greek lion now anyway?

The Greek had a knack for showing up when I thought he was out of my life for good. At this point, I equated my relationship with him to having a puppy. The puppy is forgiven for bad behavior because he's adorable. Yes, he was my puppy and I was an idiot.

As I was packing my things, ugly crying because I had to leave, and vulnerable, I saw my phone light up. I groaned. Did I want to answer this?

While I hate to admit it, I wanted to see him before I moved.

"Hi, Greek," I said.

"Did I surprise you?"

"Well, yeah. It's been a while."

"Didn't I tell you I'd call?" he said.

And so the conversation went before he asked if he could come over.

I know now I had an image of him in my head that he simply didn't or couldn't fit, but again, much like the puppy, I was so distracted by his undeniable cuteness. I got sucked in all over again.

I began the ritual of showering and shaving all things hairy - I swear, the hair maintenance never ends. Then I changed clothes a thousand times while I downed gulps of wine. Just then the buzzer sounded. I jumped!

I buzzed him up, then stood in the doorway, much like the first time I met him at my apartment.

Alexandros came up the stairs, a bottle of wine in his hand. And while I kicked myself on the inside for allowing him to come over, I still melted. He had gained some weight, but I thought it looked good on him.

He came in, setting the wine bottle on the counter, smiled, and told me I looked good. He'd always said that ala Rocky Balboa style.

"You look good, Erin."

"Thanks."

We stared at each other for a moment knowing what the other was thinking. Wow, we had chemistry. I felt myself sweating. I had dressed fast after the shower and hadn't put on deodorant yet. My plan was to get him out of my place before ripping off my sweaty clothes.

We walked to Astoria Park and the conversation was easy. It always was. There was never an awkward pause. It made me wonder why he always had to fight our closeness.

We sat on a park bench and talked; it somehow led to our parents. He shared with me how he'd finally stood up to his father who had left him, his mother, and sister when Alexandros was a teenager. The relationship with his father never sounded good, but he'd only ever shared bits and pieces.

We walked back to my house and I realized I had sweat through my tank top. I was so embarrassed, but he put me at ease by telling me that pheromones were sexy. Nice save, Greek.

I went into my room and changed into a lighter, looser top. When I came out, he was reading something I had written in grad school.

"Erin, how do you come up with this stuff? You're hilarious!"

It was in those moments when I saw his sincerity and wished to know him better. He was a closed book and only shared a chapter with me once in a while.

We read the monologue I had written. It was an aggressive German gymnast who was doing a cooking show and using athletic metaphors. Alexandros read it in his best German accent. I was laughing so hard. Then he grabbed another piece of paper.

"Here, read this with me," he said.

We read the scene together, both laughing all the way through it.

Then he stepped behind me and asked if I'd read the rest of it to him. I felt his fingertips find my stomach. He caressed me and kissed my neck.

I ducked away from him, but he grabbed my hands. We started to dance.

Who was this man and how come I had to be in love with him?

I could see him coming in for a kiss, but he didn't wait for me to lean in. He grabbed me, pulled me toward him, and kissed me, passionately.

Oh, forget it. I gave up into his embrace. Every time this man was near, my resolve was over.

We kissed and danced and danced and kissed. Then, when the neighbors pounded on the wall for us to stop making so much noise, we sat on my bedroom floor (because I'd sold all the furniture), giggling. He looked around at the empty space.

"Do you really have to leave New York, Erin?"

"I do," I said firmly. For a second, I thought I saw sadness in his eyes.

"Can I call you while you're in Wisconsin?" he asked.

"Of course." That question surprised me. I figured it was just something he said. I didn't know if I'd ever hear from him again after that night.

* * *

I landed in Wisconsin for the summer. My plan was to work for my friend, Mary during the summer and go back to New York in autumn. The summer flew by. I was teaching dance and theatre to students of all ages and having a blast. While it was weird not to be in New York, I thought it was a nice respite from the city, plus I was still working in my field.

Mary's performing arts school was thriving at the time. It was wonderful to immerse myself in that positive energy.

Some days were harder than others, as at any job. One day in particular proved rather difficult. We had a new girl just show up for one of the performing arts camps. She wasn't enrolled, her mother just dropped her off and left, leaving Mary and me wondering how this would work with two full camps.

The girl was a handful, picking fights with other children within the first hour of her arrival and even biting one of the older children who had been acting as a helper. After the biting incident, Mary called her mother to pick her up. The girl responded by screaming and telling Mary that she was not to call her mother or tell her what she'd done.

I felt sorry for the little girl. Both Mary and I knew this behavior wasn't innate in children, it's learned. I also felt for the mother who was probably trying her best.

By this point, the other students were so upset nobody was participating in any of the activities. Our next stop that afternoon was a local museum. Mary asked me if I could take the children and she'd stay with the little girl until her mother arrived.

I agreed, and headed to the museum with the students, trying to lighten the mood. At the end of the afternoon as I headed home, worn out, my phone beeped. Much to my surprise it was my Greek lion. He had called and left a message.

His voice sounded calm as he asked how I was.

Then he said, "You're probably at your job right now working miracles."

That day I'd wished I could have performed a miracle or two. Our phone conversation that evening started a turn in our relationship.

He started to call me on a regular basis. The calls often lasted an hour or two. There was never an awkward moment of silence. He was more open than ever. I wasn't sure if it was because they're was safety in the distance or something else, but whatever it was, our friendship grew in a way I'd never expected.

September came. I felt New York pulling me back, but there was the same problem there always was. Money.

I had told Clay that I wanted to come back but didn't have a place to stay or a job. I had, however, saved enough money to go to New York in October or November and stay until Christmas.

Shortly after I texted Clay I received a Facebook message from Sasha. We had never been that close while I was at Tisch, not due to any shortage of effort on her part. She intimidated the hell out of me. Because of that, I kept her at arm's length, except for the one time I let her stay at my apartment for the weekend. We wound up becoming closer that weekend than ever before and I saw her for who she is - a compassionate, strong woman who'd give anyone the shirt off her back. She told me in the message that I was welcome to stay with her. I was stunned. Without even thinking, I messaged her back. I was headed to New York in a month.

    Dorothy Never Got Down Like This

Sasha lived in Prospect Park in Brooklyn. She posted a message on Facebook with a picture of the Brooklyn welcome sign on the highway inviting me back to New York.

Chapter Nineteen

Dorothy Goes Home

Much against my family's wishes, I repacked and headed back to the Big Apple. None of them knew what I was doing and neither did I. I had no job and no prospects, but I told them it would be easier to find a job in New York than it would be in Wisconsin. And I was right.

Within the first week, Clay called and offered me a job at the same company I'd been fired from in a different department of the company. He was employed there as the boss' assistant. He said he needed someone to work in the studios, greeting the actors, preparing the studios for the actors, etc.

My reaction to going back into that same building again after being fired was much less than thrilling, but Sasha was kind enough to let me stay with her. I felt it only right to offer her some money for rent so I wanted to find a job ASAP.

When I arrived at the airport on my return, Clay agreed to meet me. I sailed down the escalator and saw him. He saw me and pursed his lips together as if he was holding in a laugh. I leaped at him and hugged him as if he was my long lost brother. He laughed and told me he couldn't get over how thin I was. I lost weight? Who knew?

We proceeded to hit one of our favorite spots for dinner before heading to Brooklyn to Sasha's place.

After we ate, we hopped on the subway. Clay told me about my new route. It was really the same as my old route from Queens, just in the opposite direction. My heart was still in Astoria, but I was happy to experience a new burrow.

By the time we stepped off the train, the sun had set. We walked in the quiet neighborhood and I immediately felt at home. A good sign. We passed lovely old brownstones and homes. Then, we crossed a bridge that went over the expressway and stood in front of the building I was about to call home.

"I'm warning you," Clay said, "it doesn't look like much on the inside."

Home is where you are.

We stepped in and the building did appear unkempt, but then again, a lot of apartments in New York looked that way. We got to the second floor and Clay knocked.

Sasha opened the door, her broad, beaming smile and open arms welcoming me. Our friend Sandra was there, too, and it was like a small Tisch reunion.

I had bought a T-shirt for Sasha with a popular TV show on the front, knowing she'd get a kick out of it. I sat down on the small bean-shaped couch and settled in, realizing it wasn't just for a weekend. I was back in New York, but this time there was no safe NYU bubble or full-time job keeping me afloat.

I took a deep breath and told myself it would be okay, as it always was. God always took good care of me wherever I went.

It wasn't long before I was working again. I agreed to work at the studios and stuffed my pride down as I stepped into the building. I settled into my new position. I wasn't there long before my friend, Erika offered me a job working at Theatre

Row in the box office. It was part-time, but it would be a good balance between my other job. In a matter of two weeks, friends not only let me stay with them, but also got me not one but two jobs. I was very grateful.

Not only had my friends helped me get back on my feet, they all came to visit me. All but one - Alexandros.

We had spent the summer getting to know each other and speaking once a week on the phone for hours. But suddenly, now that I was in New York I felt him back away yet again. What was he so afraid of?

He called me one night and told me he had lost yet another job waiting tables. I sympathized with him and tried to offer some ideas for solutions. This was a pattern with him. He had graduated with his bachelor's degree in health sciences that May. He said he wanted to work in that field; he just didn't know in what capacity.

As I tried to help him figure it out, he asked me how my job hunt was going.

I told him I had two jobs and expected a *congratulations* from him, but instead received silence.

"Wow, you come back here and get two jobs in two weeks," he said, "and I can't even keep a job. I grew up here."

It seemed as if he was threatened by me, which I never understood. I tried to change the subject, asking him when I would see him.

"What's with all the pressure, Erin?" he asked.

"Nothing. I thought it'd be nice to see each other. That's all." I backed down.

That brave lion I had come to know over the summer had disappeared and now I was left with a cowardly one.

During that conversation with Alexandros, he made it clear he didn't want to see me, even after I told him all of my friends had already visited me. When he gave me another excuse as to why he couldn't get to Brooklyn I told him to forget about it. We had an argument and I hung up. This was another pattern with us.

Soon after that conversation, Clay took matters in his own hands. He was sick of listening to me whine about the Greek. He sat me down one night in front of a computer screen and forced me to sign up on an online dating site.

I was a big believer that these websites were bullshit, probably because I'd only ever met creepers on them. But Clay was filling in the questions for me, so I acquiesced and took over.

I took the time to answer everything exactly as I would answer if I were in a conversation with someone I knew well. I wanted to be exactly who I was so whoever wanted to message me would have an idea of the *real* me - not that anybody ever reads profiles.

It took about an hour to fill out the profile. After it posted to the site, I started getting responses immediately. I was stunned!

The next day, much to my surprise, I was bombarded with messages. Clay told me to respond to everyone so I would have a lot of men to choose from.

I started with a handsome man named José. His profile pic was of him and his daughter. I was pleasantly surprised by his witty message and response to my photos, so I sent him a message. We texted for a day or two before finally calling each other. We seemed to gel and he asked to take me to dinner.

When we had the date and time confirmed, he confessed that he wasn't as tall as he said he was on his profile. I had dated shorter guys in the past and it never bothered me, and I explained my feelings to him. He sounded relieved and we moved on.

The night of our meeting came. He took me out to eat at a Mexican restaurant in my neighborhood. I was so excited to have a date I went out and bought a new dress. It was silver and nearly see-through. I had lost a lot of weight on my return to New York because I couldn't afford to eat as much as I had in Wisconsin. I felt confident in that dress. I also strapped on a pair of red boots I had purchased while going to NYU.

I felt fabulous as I made my way off the subway and toward the restaurant. I hoped my heels wouldn't make a difference to José. It was then I realized he had never told me how tall he actually was.

I shrugged it off, telling myself it didn't matter.

I stepped into the restaurant and saw him sitting in the window. I smiled and went over to greet him. Then he stood up. I think he came up to my bellybutton. I never thought height made a difference, but I have to admit this time seemed awkward. Me, feeling like the Jolly Green Giant next to tiny Papa Smurf.

There was another man I met online who said he had thinning hair, which he explained was the reason why he was wearing a baseball cap in his profile picture. Oddly enough, when I met him, I noticed he didn't lie about his thinning hair. I just didn't know his definition of thinning hair meant completely *bald*. And to be fair, I wouldn't have minded. It was more his lying about it that turned me off.

Although we looked ridiculous together, I continued to see José on and off. I don't know why I was trying to make it work. I thought of Alexandros often but hadn't heard from him since we hung up on each other.

After weeks of silence, one night he texted me.

I'm sorry, he said.

He had never apologized before. It was progress. I knew he wasn't where I was in our relationship, but I wanted to still talk to him, keep the lines of communication open.

One evening after speaking with José on the phone I got a call from the Greek. He was concerned about me. I explained what was happening with my relationship with José and he said, "Oh. I'm that guy now?"

I wasn't sure what Alexandros meant.

"*What* guy?" I asked.

"A guy you talk to about your *other* relationships."

I paused and made a conscious effort to think about my response before I answered. He was the one who'd always made it clear he wasn't ready for anything more than friendship.

"You mean *this* matters to you?" I asked.

"Of course, it matters to me. I don't want to talk to you about a guy you're seeing."

"Why?" I prodded, fishing for more information and

hoping he'd bite.

"Because it bothers me, Erin. I know you'll find someone some day and I suppose… Well, I suppose it will bother me when you do."

I took a deep breath, then spit out the words I should've kept to myself. "It's you, you know. It's always been you."

"What do you mean?" he asked.

"It's you, you stupid idiot! It's you that I'm waiting for. It's you that I want to be with. It's you that I…"

I stopped myself. I couldn't say it. If I said the words out loud it'd hurt even more.

"That you what, Erin?" It was his turn to prod me.

I shrugged, though being on the phone he couldn't see my reaction. "Nothing. It doesn't matter."

"That you *love*?"

"Don't make me say it, Alexandros. You know how I feel," I said flatly.

"I know what you want, but I'm not in a place where I can give that commitment to you. I don't have any money to be someone's boyfriend."

"Why does it always come down to money with you?" I asked.

It didn't matter to me. I wanted a relationship. Period. But his issues ran much deeper than his financial deficiency. Being the Dorothy that I was I ignored his words and held an optimistic image of him in my head.

In hindsight, I wish I would've listened to what he was trying to share with me that night. He was telling me the truth - that he couldn't give me what I wanted – a relationship. He wasn't cowardly at all - he was honest.

* * *

I returned to New York in November that year. Things were working well with my two part-time jobs. I was barely making ends meet, but I was content for the moment. Sasha and I got closer. We would cook for each other, watch TV and movies together, and I'd kill the roaches in her apartment with my tap shoes. (So much for taking a tap class.)

At the end of January, things shifted abruptly. Sasha's health was in question and she started to retreat within herself. Try as I may to ask what I could do to help her, she reminded me that it wasn't about me. While I understood what she meant, I felt hurt she was suddenly pushing me away, especially since all I really wanted to do was help.

Then in February it was announced our hours would be cut at the studio. Nothing was working out, and I pondered again just what to do. I was barely making enough to pay her the $500 each month she asked for in rent and now, with less hours, my pay checks would be smaller. My second time around in New York seemed - much to my surprise - to be up. It was as if the universe was telling me, "There's nothing left for you here."

Alexandros had made little effort to see me. I don't know why I was surprised by this, but I was.

I had moved back before Thanksgiving and it wasn't until days before Christmas I had a call from him, letting me know he was in Brooklyn and wanted to meet up. I was coming from work and in my crazy distraction took the wrong train home. I don't think I was ever so manic in my life. I had become one of those women I can't stand, someone who drops everything for a guy who barely gives her the time of day.

We were meeting at the Court Street stop next to the Christmas tree. I was standing there in my red coat feeling incredibly beautiful. I don't know if it was the larger-than-life Christmas tree or the brisk New York air, or the excitement of knowing I was about to see him. I stood admiring the tree. I saw someone coming toward me dressed in all black and a hoodie.

Squinting, I thought it must be Alexandros. As he finally came into view, he smiled that cocky smile, opened his arms and embraced me, giving me a peck on the cheek as he always did. His presence was enormous.

I wanted to hide under his hoodie and stay with him. He was my protector.

We walked around an area of Brooklyn I hadn't been in before. That was always one of my favorite parts of New York - getting off the subway at a stop I'd never been to before and discovering a whole new world. It was especially idyllic in the city with everything lit up for Christmas.

I was starving, so we stopped in a restaurant. I ducked into the bathroom. When I returned, he had taken the booth end of the table facing the rest of the dining room. He looked comfortable.

I moved to sit down on the chair facing him.

He said, "I'm sorry, Erin, do you want to come over here and sit with me?"

I smiled and slid in next to him. I was looking at the menu when he confessed to me that he had very little money. This was a regular problem with him. I shrugged and told him not to worry about it.

When the burger came, I cut it in half and we sat together, sharing the plate and catching up on what had happened over the last few months. The time and distance fell away easily, and it was as if we'd never been apart.

While I enjoyed the return of his closeness, I knew there was still a wall there that, no matter how close we became, there was a part of him I couldn't reach. I should've stopped trying; I would've saved myself a lot of hurt.

When we finished our meal, I paid the tab and we walked to the subway. He hugged me and headed down to the platform, leaving in the opposite direction. I saw him get on his train and my eyes teared up, not knowing how long it would be before I'd see him again.

As I wiped away a tear, I realized I had to get over Alexandros. As much as I hated to admit it, I loved him much more than he loved me. It was that horrible, unrequited, sickly kind of love that made me want to throw up in my mouth a little bit.

I spent February and March trying to make a plan of how to stay in New York. I was still seeing José and Sai, the bald man, but not seriously on either count. They both wanted me to move in with them. It seemed like an awfully big leap since we had only gone on a few dinner dates together and I barely knew either one of them. Not to mention, I was still in love with Alexandros.

I also had something strange going on physically with

my body. I thought I was dying. I'd been having horrible back and stomach pains. When I searched online for my symptoms (which you should never do) it pointed to ovarian cancer. That scared me, but I didn't have any insurance at the time. I figured I'd have to go to Wisconsin eventually to see my primary physician. So I did that.

I didn't have ovarian cancer. Turns out I was just super constipated. I was full of shit for real - *fabulous*.

In March, after nothing came of any permanent jobs I'd applied for, I knew I had to give Sasha notice. I arranged for a flight back to the Dairy State on March 31st. This felt so final to me in a way that I hadn't felt before. I checked in with my heart again. It was telling me it was okay to leave.

I found a job in childcare back in Wisconsin. I spent my summer changing diapers - something that was never on my list of things I ever wanted to do at a job - and wondering why I had worked so hard to move to New York and get my degree.

It wasn't long before I'd lost all hope. I remembered the day when I spoke with Laura, the Chair of the Graduate Musical Theatre Writing Department, for my Tisch interview. When I'd hung up I thought if I went to grad school there, I'd graduate, and the world would open up with opportunities. Then, what would happen? For a brief moment, my thoughts became dark. *What if nothing happens and you have to go back to Wisconsin?* Which is exactly what happened, until two monumental opportunities came knocking.

Chapter Twenty

Back in Kansas – or Wisconsin

I had applied for a teaching job at a local Wisconsin college - something I really wanted to do. I'd been rejected in June.

In July, they contacted me again to say that the person they hired had backed out and was I still interested?

Was I still interested? Hell yes, I was still interested! That was the first astonishing thing to happen to me since I'd been back in my home state.

The second amazing thing that happened I never saw coming. It was by far the most startling thing that has ever happened to me.

I came home from work one day after being up to my elbows in diapers. I sat down on the sofa, sick, tired, and stressed. I noticed I had an email on my phone from the Yale School of Drama. Soyhun and I had applied to their musical development workshop with *Out of the Blue* but didn't get accepted. That was months ago, so I couldn't imagine what this email was about.

When I read it, I nearly fell off of my chair. It was from someone who was involved in the musical theatre development program. She had a request from one of the judges of the festival, who was a well-known Broadway actress and Tony winner. The request went something like this:

Dear Erin and Soyhun,

Last year you submitted your piece, Out of the Blue, *to the Institute. One of our readers is interested in contacting you regarding that work. Would it be all right with you if I pass on your information to her? Or alternatively, could I pass on her information to you and you can reach out if you'd like? Please let me know your thoughts.*

I was shocked! The woman had been nominated for three more Tonys. She liked our musical? I couldn't believe it.

I emailed Soyhun who, as usual, remained completely underwhelmed which was a nice balance to my complete lunacy. I'd done a happy dance in my bathroom twice.

A few months later, we received this email from our Broadway star.

Hi Erin and Soyhun!

Thanks for contacting me. I wanted to begin a dialogue with you two because when I was a reader for YIMT, your piece absolutely knocked me out. It was my favorite of all the pieces I read, and I was quite moved by the story and the writing. Your level of craft is impressive and of course, as point of view and perspective are everything, I appreciated the humor and wit of it all so much.

If you are interested, I would love for you to send me a copy of your script, score, and MP3 files, if you have them, so I can have a second look. Readers do not have access to your material after we submit our scores. As soon as we hit send, the material evaporates! So I would love to read and listen again, and then set up a time to meet or talk. My hope would be that if we click, maybe we could discuss my coming on board as a collaborator in a director capacity, if you are not already working with someone. If you are, I can just be a fan and supporter of your work! I am also happy to contact your agents or representation, if you prefer.

I read it and then laughed - I love that she thought we had representation. But suddenly it felt like the world was reaching for us. This was a whole new experience.

The next four years of my life were really weird. Weird in that sort of unexpected, unpredictable way that gets your hopes up. I equate it to Dorothy walking down that long hallway with her cohorts to meet the wizard for the first time, except I was walking the hallway alone. I wished for a Scarecrow to hold onto. Thank God Clay was in New York to catch me when I finally came to the end of my own yellow brick road. This was probably the biggest roller coaster I was on and something inside me told me that either I was going to fly successfully off the cliff or land face down on the bottom of the rocks. I hoped for the first, because the second sounded painful and rather messy.

Before I went to NYU I had one of those gut feelings I tend to get like I had when I met the Greek. I know once I have them, whatever I'm sensing is guaranteed to come true. I don't know if this is some kind of compass God placed in my brain like a microchip that pushes me forward or just a premonition, but while I consider it a gift, it can also be a curse. I was 100 percent sure that there would be one person who would like our musical, champion it, and move it forward. So when we received the email from this incredibly talented woman, I was sure it would be her.

It was November, 2014 when Soyhun and I met her in person. I had talked to her on the phone a few times and she had intimidated me. Not because she wasn't kind - she was incredibly so. I knew how much I wanted to be *like* her. I admired her strength and sensibility, as well as her openness. What famous director takes the time to help out no-name writers? I kept asking myself that. Why would she want to help us?

She was directing *A Light in the Piazza* at Pace University in New York. She had invited us to come see her work. Even today, it still seems unreal to me.

I was directing at St. Norbert College in Wisconsin, but luckily it was the weekend after opening so I was free to fly to New York to see the show. Soyhun and I talked, and we agreed I would stay with her. We'd go to the show together, meet her afterwards, and talk about our piece.

As I arrived in New York, my eyes teared up. It had been six long months since I left and I wasn't sure if or when I'd live there ever again. I missed it as much as Dorothy missed Kansas.

I met Soyhun at her new place in Sunnyside. It was adorable. I was happy to see her. Still, our collaboration felt strained. We both knew it, too. I think we both knew that if we were going to take our musical to Broadway it'd be a lot of blood, sweat, and tears. The common ground we found was that we both believed in the piece and that kept us going.

We headed together to Pace University that night. I wore a black, tight fitting dress and I was so nervous I was sweating. I was a hot mess.

     Dorothy Never Got Down Like This

We watched the show. We got a text from the director that said she was on her way to the theatre and would be there after the show, so we should meet her in the lobby.

I always play something out in my mind before it happens. I have a specific way of how I think it should go, and most often, reality isn't anything like it.

As I was applauding the students at the end of the show, my nerves came back over meeting this Broadway star and Tony winner in person. I imagined seeing her, then running up and giving her a big hug. *Erin, that's insane. Don't do that.*

Soyhun and I went into the lobby where a crowd of people huddled around someone. We looked and looked for her but didn't see her. That is, until the crowd slowly dissipated, and I saw a puff of blond hair and a light that shown from her.

I swallowed hard and tried to collect myself. I felt my lip quiver and wetness under my arms. More sweat? What was with the sweat?

I looked down and realized Soyhun and I were standing next to a garbage can. I laughed to myself. *Here we are, the no-name writers, standing next to garbage.*

The director saw us and Soyhun gave her a little wave. She tried to make her way toward us, but more fans grabbed her attention. I watched it all, thinking how incredible she was. She was on Broadway, directing a show, teaching workshops, and found time to talk with nearly each and every person who came up to her. I was so in awe of this woman that when she made her way over to us I did the one thing I told myself *not* to do. I hugged her. I couldn't help it. I was so grateful to her that I lost myself for a second.

She remained very composed.

I tried to pull myself together, but Soyhun, who is ever calm and collected, began speaking with her about our show. She told us about the first time she read it, describing the judging process at Yale.

"Do you know how it works?" she asked.

"We don't know anything," I said. (Yes, I really said that.)

"Well," she said, "you have to score every question from 1 through 10 and when I read *Out of the Blue* I was like 10, 10, 10!" Her enthusiasm for our piece was contagious.

She went on to explain that she doesn't ever listen to the music first. She only reads the libretto. She liked what she read so much that she listened to the music.

I had to let those words sink in for a second - that she liked my script and lyrics and Soyhun's music that much that she wanted more. I spent so much time telling myself how much I sucked at lyric writing that to hear her positive words set my brain on tilt. It was as if someone was tapping me on the shoulder telling me I was *worthy*. If only I'd listen.

The meeting was brief. She told us that she had a producer who was willing to produce whatever show she was interested in directing so we could meet and talk again in February after she returned from Africa where she'd be working on another project.

I didn't know when the woman slept. She said she would contact us in a few months, then she turned around to see to her fans.

Soyhun and I continued to stand there - next to the garbage

can - not knowing what to do. Do we leave or try to talk to her again?

I think her turning her back on us was our cue to go, but we didn't know for sure. I tried to say something else but as soon as the last person stepped away from her, she disappeared into the theatre. It happened so fast.

As I watched her go, I thought about her presence. *It must take so much energy to do what she did.* I couldn't imagine holding it together for that long, yet she remained composed and calm. I, on the other hand, had a live wire feeling. I needed to get out of the building fast and take a deep breath.

Soyhun and I stepped outside and started our walk toward NYU. We were meeting a friend at Josie Woods. Soyhun had a way of grounding me. I found it a little annoying, but truthfully, she was right. I was so excited my head was in the clouds. I could've been sitting on top of the Empire State Building.

Soyhun remained on the ground. "We never know, Erin. This doesn't mean anything."

As much as I hated to admit it, she was right.

It wasn't until nearly midnight on the last day in February 2015 that I was about to give up when we got an email from our perspective director. I was in bed still awake and trying to catch up on things when I saw her email come through my inbox. I nearly fell on the floor. She was incredibly busy doing previews for *Gigi* on Broadway and had asked if she could pitch our piece to theatres in New York to get a reading for us.

It was surreal.

I emailed her back and thanked her, copied Soyhun, and

let the director know I'd get back to her as soon as I heard from Soyhun, but I'm sure we'd be thrilled to have her do that for us.

I sat there, stunned. It seemed too good to be true. I thanked God. I felt blessed that we had her in our corner. I could see my life unfolding as I pictured it. *Out of the Blue* was about to become a reality.

Fast forward to March 2015.

Our director asked us to gather materials together and send them to her. She was meeting with theaters regarding our show. She started with Playwrights Horizons, a writer's theatre that did original works. She was meeting with the artistic director there - he had also directed my 20-minute musical with Clay while we were at Tisch, but who knew if he'd remember me.

Turns out he didn't, or at least he didn't remember reading our musical. Soyhun and I had sent *Out of the Blue* to him for a recommendation letter so we could apply to one of the New York Musical festivals.

Our director called me at the end of March to let me know what happened with the meetings, but not to worry. She'd find the right theatre.

"It's all about finding the right fit," she said.

I really believed in her and knew she believed in us.

She approached a few more theatres. We heard a lot of so-so rejections. "We like it, but…"

Our director confided to us that even John Kander was hearing no's. I guess if one of the most famous musical theatre writers can't get a reading, who are we to think we could.

Our director was starring in a show on Broadway, getting married, and in the midst of all of this, she invited us to come, hang out at her house, and read through our piece. We could talk about it. Again, I felt so blessed that we had this amazing woman in our corner. I spoke with her on the phone, hung up, and ordered my plane ticket to New York. Hopping on a flight and going back over the rainbow.

Chapter Twenty-one

Dorothy is a cock-eyed optimist

There's a scene in *The Wizard of Oz* when the balloon leaves without Dorothy. I first saw this scene as a child and wondered *how is she going to get home now?* She wanted to go home. She was willing to go. I don't think I understood the reason for my constant want to return to Wisconsin until after I'd experienced the same type of turning point in my life. I thought I knew what I wanted before I moved to New York. I thought I knew what was best for me, but sometimes the journey is there to simply redirect us. That was what was about to happen to me, but not before a shit ton of disappointment.

My flight to New York was leaving on Wednesday, August 5th, 2015. I was staying until Tuesday the following week. I was so excited for Soyhun and I to meet with our director and discuss our musical that I could barely keep from giggling at any given moment.

Then there was the matter of the Greek.

Through all of the arguing, ignoring, phone flirting, and wondering over the last year of why this man was still in my life I knew I had to stand strong in my promise to him - that I wouldn't contact him while I was there visiting. I was not going to beg for his attention like I had done in the past. If he wanted to see me, he would have to contact me.

I hadn't seen him for over a year and a half, but while I was in Wisconsin I'd felt like we'd grown closer. The last time

I'd seen him in the flesh had been the day we parted on the subway in Brooklyn. After that day, he called me at least once a week and we would talk, really talk about our lives. This, of course, was after a huge fight we had and didn't speak for five months, the longest stretch of time not speaking. Oddly enough, when I look back, I'm not sure what the fights were about. I think it boiled down to the fact that he was afraid of commitment and I was pushing too hard for that.

On my birthday in June, I didn't hear from him and it hurt. He always remembered my birthday. He called me a few days later and left me a message apologizing for not calling me.

I called him back and we talked for hours. Despite everyone in my life telling me how bad this man was for me, I still believed he was right for me, even though there was a big part of me that wished I could just move on without him. That part was the sensible, grounded 3.5% of me that I normally choose to ignore.

I told him on the phone I was coming to visit. I said very clearly, "I'd like to see you, Alexandros, but I'll leave that up to you."

He's an odd animal, a squirrel living in a bear's body. If I made any sudden movements, he'd dart up a tree. I promised myself I wouldn't make any more effort for him. It was his turn now and I meant it.

I flew out on Wednesday, August 5th. The weather was calm, I felt peaceful. Life was good.

I stepped out of the airport to get a cab and took a deep breath of the gritty New York air. *I'm back home.*

I got in a cab and could tell the cab driver was a bit green.

He ended up asking me for directions of where I wanted to go, and I gave them. The New Yorker in me hadn't left.

The cabbie dropped me off in Astoria and I met Soyhun's roommate in front of the apartment where I was staying for a few days. I had plans to meet Soyhun in Sunnyside to get a key from her. Later, I settled in my room, which was spacious and furnished with an air conditioner. I was so happy to be back in Astoria. I'd missed it.

I hopped on the subway and it was as if I'd never left. I took the N train to the 7 train and got off in Sunnyside. Soyhun had a knack for finding these lovely little neighborhoods with cute places to live. Her apartment was right off of a main stop near the train. We were meeting at a nearby diner. I had arrived first and waited for her.

When I saw her come in, she was completely adorable at seven months pregnant. I hadn't seen her since November. It was so good to see her beaming with life. We talked a lot and got our plan together for meeting with our director, then caught up on other things.

The next morning when I awoke I felt like an electrical chord with no outlet. I had so much energy. That day we would be spending at our director's house - a Tony winner. How in God's name did that happen? I was so nervous. I was hoping my charming, breezy demeanor wouldn't run for the door when I met her. When that happens, it usually leaves this gawky, awkward Wisconsin girl who can't form a sentence. Soyhun, on the other hand, is always charming, so at least one of us had our head on straight.

At our director's apartment, she invited us in and immediately made us feel at home. She's an incredibly elegant woman inside and out with a kind energy. I'm rarely intimidated by people, but I had a hard time looking her in the eyes. Her gaze is so strong and powerful - in a good way. As if nothing could stop her. I admire that kind of strength in a person. I knew if our musical was going to go anywhere it was going to because of the strength that she, I, and Soyhun had all together. The triad is unstoppable.

We spent the day with our director, reading and singing through our musical.

She is such an incredible actress that when she would read a scene with me, I'd get caught up in observing her and forget where I left off in the script. After we read through it, we went up on the rooftop of her building and she gave us notes on our piece. I looked around at the Hudson to our right with a large sailboat passing through, reminding me of my hometown, Sturgeon Bay. Up on the rooftop, Washington Heights, New York was peaceful and serene.

The next morning, we met with the artistic director at The Public Theatre. It was opening week for the new musical *Hamilton*, and our director had met with her previously before our meeting and spoke about our piece. I'm sure because of this meeting the artistic director wanted to give us feedback.

That morning, as I rushed to get organized, I had an out of body experience. Something told me that it didn't matter what happened. I was so grateful to be having this experience - to have a mentor working with us and for us, and to be meeting with The Public Theatre. Soyhun and I couldn't believe it. It still didn't seem real.

We met at the Public and heard our feedback. It was similar to the feedback our director gave us which, essentially, was that we had a strong foundation for *Out of the Blue* but needed to heighten the stakes for our main character, Jenny.

After the meeting ended, we left. Standing in the elevator on our way down to the ground floor, I looked over at our director and felt as if I was about to start crying uncontrollably. Her belief in our work and in *us* was rare - I didn't know how to express my gratitude. I hugged her and thanked her and told her I was so excited I might pee.

She hugged me back and said, "You should be excited, but don't pee."

Soyhun and I took her to lunch. Still, it felt surreal. Observing her, she is so down-to-earth, it was easy to feel comfortable around her. We walked to the subway with her and we gave her a hug. As we walked behind her, I looked up, seeing her, dressed all in white, her blond hair up in a clip. She emoted this light of beauty, grace, and power.

I could see myself the same way in the future.

On the train on the way back, Soyhun and I went through our usual discussion of how we were going to rewrite the show with life happening - with her having a baby soon and me teaching in Wisconsin. Tisch may have been grueling, but all we had to focus on while we were there was writing our musical.

I tried to reassure Soyhun that we would make it work. I knew she was nervous, and frankly, so was I. We had people reviewing our work. Really looking at it as a viable musical for production, which is scary as hell.

I got off the subway, went back to the apartment and sat on the bed. I wept for about 15 minutes, not quite sure why.

I was confused and overwhelmed, but in a good way. As I was lying there, I knew what I needed. I needed someone to hug me for a really long time.

I thought of Alexandros with his deep brown eyes. I wanted to see him, but I figured he'd call me on Sunday, the day before I left.

I tried to relax, wondering when everything would come to fruition; when our musical would be produced, if ever. When, if ever, would I live in New York again? When would the man I love be willing to love me back? I checked in with my heart again - it was about to burst.

I had to stop. I took a deep breath and let it all go. Instead, I decided to get up and shower and go for a walk in my favorite neighborhood.

It felt good to let the hot water splash against my closed eyelids. I thought of my grandfather and wondered if he would be proud of me.

I got out of the shower, toweled off, and threw on a flowered summer dress, then stepped out into Astoria. I wandered up and down Broadway, looking for something to eat but not settling on any one thing. I reached into my purse to check my phone messages and saw Alexandros was calling at that very minute. I missed answering the call, so I called him back.

It was good to hear his voice. He asked where I was. I told him, and he laughed.

"Guess where I am? I'm on Steinway Street," he said.

Steinway intersects with Broadway. Amazing. He told me that he had just finished work and had a feeling it was a good time to call me.

I told him it was perfect timing and we decided to meet on the corner.

As I headed toward Steinway, I felt butterflies swirling around in my stomach, my body felt electric. I couldn't wait to see him. It had been over a year, and although we talked at least once a week, I couldn't wait to look into his eyes again or touch him.

I stood on the corner waiting, trying to look casual, but inside, my heart was doing cartwheels. It felt like an eternity waiting there.

I saw him coming toward me. He was crossing the street and didn't see me staring at him. He had this huge grin on his face. I noticed he had lost close to 30 pounds. He looked taller and incredibly fit. And so fricking hot!

I swallowed hard, like on the first day I saw him come up the stairs to my apartment. I braced myself for his larger than life presence.

He saw me, said my name, kissed me, then hugged me for a really long time. Embracing him felt so good. I had missed him more than I could ever recall missing anyone.

We stopped hugging and caught our breath. It was as if we were both so happy to see one another that we didn't know what to say to each other. He put his arm around me and we started to walk.

"Erin, I can't believe you're here."

I couldn't speak. I squeezed his hand in reply.

We got halfway down the street and he asked me if I wanted an iced coffee. I nodded.

We darted into Dunkin' Donuts. He said he'd order me something wonderful. I trusted him, and he did. When he paid for the order I realized it was the first time he'd bought me anything. That small gesture felt nice and new. I remembered the first frappe he brought me, which was three-quarters gone when he handed it to me. He was treating me differently.

He asked where I was staying.

I told him we could walk there, and I'd show him. My brain went to sex and his may have, too, but I decided I was just going to show him the place and leave.

We strolled down Broadway and went to the apartment. We sat on the bed in the room where I was staying and talked. I rested my head on his chest and he put his arms around me. He held me for what seemed like a long time, but not long enough.

I allowed myself to relax into his arms and all the anxiety of the day faded away. I closed my eyes and did what I always did when I was with him. I thanked God for the moment, as long as it lasted. I believed he was the other half of me and to be near him again was comforting.

I couldn't believe how this man's presence made me feel. To be fair, I hadn't had sex in what felt like years.

I stood up and sat in a chair across the room from him because there was no way I was sleeping with him. I wanted to, though. With every fiber of my being, I wanted to tear his clothes off and be on top of him. I decided against it. He had hurt me too many times for me to offer him the gift of myself again.

"Why are you over there, Erin?" he asked.

"It's safer. I have to be over here, because I haven't had sex in like eight years. If I continue to sit by you, we'll be having sex."

He smiled his boyish grin and it softened his hard, chiseled features.

"Well, we're both adults," he said.

"Yes, that's true." *Change the subject, Erin.* "Let's go for a walk."

We stood up and gathered our things, and headed out into the Astoria air. How I made it out of that room without having sex with him that day I don't know, but I was proud of myself for doing so.

We walked to Astoria Park. It was a park we both loved and spent a lot of time in. As we walked, we talked - as usual, there were no awkward pauses. He took my hand, lifted my arm, and spun me around. It felt as if we were in a Rom Com and I loved every minute.

In the park, we walked down by the water, which was what we had done the first night we went out four years prior. We sat close to each other on the bench and he rested his head against my chest. I wrapped my arms around him and kissed the back of his neck. His actions were calm and peaceful, more so than I could ever remember. I thought to myself that if this wasn't love, I didn't know what it was.

I could feel it from Alexandros, too. We sat like that for a while, then stood up and walked some more. We reached another bench and sat down. We kissed for a long moment.

I was kissing him like my life depended on it.

Then he leaned back and looked into my eyes.

"I don't know where you learned to kiss like that, Erin," he said. "Let me look into your eyes. I mean, really look."

He gazed into my eyes for a long time. I could see past his strength into that soft part of him - his heart, which I knew to be good and kind.

"Do you think about me when I'm not here?" I asked.

He paused, looking down at the ground.

"Well -"

"It's okay. You can be honest," I said.

"Not all the time."

"Well, you're going to think about me a lot more now," I said confidently.

He looked at me when I said that, and I think he knew I was right.

My phone went off and I saw it was a text from Clay. I was late meeting him in Midtown for a show we were going to later. Alexandros and I wandered back to the subway, all the while talking, laughing, and kissing.

When we got to the N train, he stood against a pillar underneath it and we kissed again for a long time. I pulled back and told him I loved him.

Before I could hear him say it back to me, the train went by over us.

I walked up the stairs and saw him go out of sight, not knowing when or if I would ever see him again.

The rest of that evening completed what may have been one of the best days of my life.

Clay and I went to 54 Below to see our friend and colleague, Sabrina, from Tisch. She had written her own show and it was performed that night. We saw so many of our friends from grad school, it was like a reunion.

Later, I made my way back to Astoria around 2 AM. I sat waiting for the subway doors to close while the train was stuck at Queens Borough Plaza, staring out into the New York night air, I shut my eyes to pray. I thanked God for the entire day and every moment I ever had in New York.

Chapter Twenty-two

Dorothy says Good-bye

Alexandros texted me early the next morning. Chancing it, I asked if I would see him again before I left, knowing it might make him feel threatened. Then I told him to forget I asked. I had to be grateful for the time we had and not dwell on whether or not I would see him again. It was the first time I had allowed myself to be in control. There was something very freeing about that - I felt confident about the situation in a way I hadn't been before.

Much to my surprise, Alexandros called me on Sunday night. He wanted to see me. I was walking in Midtown with Clay and I told him I was leaving the next morning. It was odd. He sounded upset that he wasn't going to get to see me again.

"I thought you were leaving on Tuesday," he said.

"No. I told you I'm leaving Monday."

"I thought it was Tuesday. I really want to see you again, Erin."

As I looked down, watching myself stride up 8th Street, I realized the shoe was suddenly on the other foot. I wasn't asking for his time, he was asking for mine.

"Well, we'll see each other again next time I come," I said confidently.

It was the first time I had ever felt in control of my emotions regarding our relationship and he seemed to take notice of the difference. His voice softened, and he tried to make an effort to get me to come see him. I was firm in my answer and told him I couldn't.

After I returned to Wisconsin I fell into a bit of a post-New York depression. Alexandros called me a couple of times. I knew what had happened between us was so special and unique, but something had changed. I prayed a lot those next few weeks for him to step up and make an effort.

Just when I was about to give up on him, I got a phone call. It was on a Sunday night. His voice was different - softer and calmer. He told me that he missed my company.

I asked him why he hadn't returned my "I love you" when we were at the subway station.

He said he had. "You just want me to say it again, you sicky."

I laughed, and told him I hadn't heard it because we were standing under a train.

Then, he told me that he loved me.

I almost screamed out loud. *Finally, finally, finally!* What had taken this man so long to admit it.

We decided we were going to try to have a relationship. We would do it long distance until we could figure out something else. I told him I would fly to New York in October for a visit and we could see how things would go.

We spent countless hours on the phone over the next two months - talking and building a relationship. I couldn't believe how constant he was. I was learning to trust him, which was big for me, because I always struggled with that in my relationships.

I bought my ticket to leave on Thursday, October 7th. He seemed so concerned over the phone, telling me that he *wished* he could pay for it. The operative word here is *wished.*

Because I was visiting him in October, I asked him to come to Wisconsin at Christmas.

That seemed to make him happy, stating that his family fought over the holidays. Really, it seemed like his family was fighting *all* the time, so I didn't see how it would be any different at Christmas.

It was nearing October and I could sense Alexandros getting nervous during our phone conversations. The one thing I knew about him was that he was terrified of commitment. The minute I told him I had bought the plane ticket I felt him begin to retreat. To add to the mix, I, too was petrified of what was happening between us. I thought I had wanted our relationship to become a reality, but in that moment, I also hit the panic button.

Everything had seemed wonderful between Alexandros and I. Why did I have this feeling in the pit of my stomach that it was about to go terribly wrong? It wasn't a sort of feeling or nervousness. It was a feeling of *you're going to come back from this trip with a totally different perspective of this man.*

My feelings of intuition never seem to be wrong, so I had to ask myself what was going to happen? How would I move on? I had to tell myself to go on the trip and see what happens. That was all I could do.

I spent so much money before I left. I got my hair dyed to

cover up the little bit of gray which was popping up. I bought a purple cotton dress that looked cute on me and would be comfortable on the plane. I even had my teeth cleaned, but I stopped myself at new shoes.

The day to fly out came and I was so excited I could barely breathe. While waiting at the airport in Wisconsin I texted Alexandros.

He said he was getting his hair cut.

Text me a picture, I asked.

I don't text selfies was his response back.

When I got off the plane, I texted him.

He responded, letting me know he was at the airport.

I had dreamed of this day, of getting off the plane at LGA and having him meet me there. I couldn't believe it was happening. As I stepped into LaGuardia Airport I realized I needed a minute to collect myself. It had been months since we'd seen each other. I darted into the bathroom, found a stall, and took a deep breath. I was shaking.

"Okay, Erin, pull yourself together," I whispered. I thought I might pass out from being so nervous.

I left the bathroom and walked towards the large glass doors, knowing that when they opened I'd travel down the escalator…and there he'd be.

As I sailed down the escalator, I scanned the area in front of me, not seeing him. I panicked, thinking he hadn't shown up. But I knew he was there. He'd texted me to tell me so.

Then I looked to my left and there he was. Standing there, looking so handsome. He appeared to be nervous, which made me feel better about my nerves.

I smiled and waited for him to walk towards me.

He didn't move, though, as if he was frozen in place.

I strolled over to him, put my things down, and said, "I'm gonna hug you now. Is that okay?"

"No," he said. "We can hug later."

He had mentioned over the phone that he wanted a long hug and told me that I could give it to him someplace secluded where we didn't have to feel self-conscious.

I wanted to hug him right away. So when his first word to me was no, it hurt. I gave him a brief embrace, but already I was disappointed. This wasn't the welcome I was hoping for.

We headed out of the airport when a lovely woman who worked there saw me and him together. She said to Alexandros, "You were waiting for this beautiful woman, and here she is."

It was the best greeting I'd ever received from a LaGuardia airport employee.

Alexandros smiled at me. "See, New York is welcoming you back, Erin."

We stepped across the street to wait for the bus. Finally, he was filled with excitement. "I can't believe you're here, Erin."

I loved it when he would look at me, really *look* at me. Staring at me as if I wasn't real, telling me how beautiful I was. I felt so blissfully happy, like I'd eaten an entire New York cheesecake and not gained an ounce. I thanked him for the prayer he sent me earlier that week. Probably one of the things I loved most about Alexandros was that I was comfortable talking to him about God.

We got on the bus and he paid for my ride. That surprised me. There were a lot of people on the bus, but he found me a seat and stood in front of me. He asked me how my flight was and we made small talk until the next stop when two seats in front of me opened up.

We sat down together and were so giddy with excitement that we didn't know what to say to each other. A young mother with two toddlers sat across from us. We couldn't help but smile and be entertained by them.

I rubbed my fingers over his arm - I had a thing for his forearms. I apologized for doing it.

He said, "No, please, touch me."

I told him how I was always happy to leave Milwaukee.

He responded, "Don't say anything bad about Wisconsin, or I won't come over Christmas." He had a smile on his face as he teased me.

I could tell he had been thinking about that response, which pleased me immensely.

It wasn't long before we were off the bus and in the warm sunshine and comfort of our favorite neighborhood. I pulled the handle out of the bottom of my small carry-on and followed him to a café.

There, he told me that he wanted to tell me about some goals he'd been thinking about for his future. This also pleased me, to think he'd want to share those things with me.

We found a cute café with outdoor seating, sat down and breathed in the autumn-scented air of the day. We ordered and made small talk as we waited. Stunning women were walking by and I noticed Alexandros was only focused on me. I was amazed by that.

He'd been considering taking the test to become a paramedic for the New York Fire Department. He was good under pressure, in fact, he was calm - he thrived in chaos. I let him know he should be doing exactly that. I was proud of him and really hoped he'd follow through with it.

When the check came, he took it and we continued to sit there and talk. Everything seemed perfect, but I still felt scared of that feeling I'd had before I left. I put the fear in the back of my mind, telling myself all would be well.

We walked to a nearby church he liked to frequent in Astoria. It was a beautiful, ornate Greek Orthodox church. He showed me how the Greeks kiss the Virgin Mary image and then kneel in front of it to pray. I enjoyed seeing him in this environment. He was more at peace than ever before.

I stepped into the archway of the church, gazing around in awe of all the images of Saints painted on the ceiling, the statues lining the walls. It was like nothing I'd ever seen before. When I turned around, Alexandros was walking toward me holding two candles in his hand.

He looked into my eyes when he handed me one, then beckoned me to a large wooden box filled with one lit candle held up by sand.

He held his candle into the flame and gestured for me to

do the same. It reminded me of that moment in a wedding ceremony when the bride and groom place their candles into one candle to signify them becoming one.

When I placed my candle into the flame, he took his out and placed it in the sand. I put mine into the sand next to his when I saw his candle lean in the other direction.

Alexandros went further into the church and I followed him. While he peered up at the ceiling, I snuck a photo of him with my phone. One of my favorite things about his eyes was that they were so big I could see the whites under the brown. I was able to capture that in the photo.

He looked over his shoulder and caught me. He didn't say anything, but I knew he hated to get his photo taken.

We sat down in a pew together. I felt closer to him in that moment than I had before. I thanked God for this time with him, but something inside me told me it was nearing an end. Again, I tried to push the thought out of my mind. I didn't understand how or why it would be coming to an end - everything was so wonderful. *Why was I feeling like this? Was I more afraid of commitment than he was?*

As more people entered the church, I felt Alexandros grow uncomfortable beside me. He leaned over to me and said, "Let's go. You know me. I don't like crowds."

And I did know him, or so I thought so that day.

We left the church and walked several blocks. I was getting tired, having just flown in, and wanted to put my bag down. I asked him if we could go to his place. We were about to head in that direction when he saw some of his friends he hadn't seen in a while sitting at an outdoor table of a pizza place.

Alexandros was so eager to introduce me to them. He introduced me to his friend, Teddy, who I could tell was older than Alexandros. He had kind eyes and a warm smile.

Teddy shook my hand and smiled at Alexandros. I felt like it was an approval.

A young Greek guy rolled up on a bike. He was jumping off and knocked knuckles with Alexandros.

Alexandros was ready to take the bike for a spin when Teddy said, "No brakes."

The men chuckled, and Alexandros handed the bike back to his friend.

We sat together at the table with another couple who lounged there. I talked to them as Alexandros chatted with Teddy. They began to speak about Teddy's girlfriend who he seemed to be having problems with. The next thing I knew they were speaking in Greek. After their tete-a-tete, Alexandros jumped up and headed toward the door of the pizza place.

"I'm going to get a slice. Erin, you want one?"

I smiled and said yes.

He went in, and as I was talking to Teddy, I could see Alexandros looking at me from inside the restaurant. I smiled, and he smiled back. He came out, handing me a piece of warm, gooey cheese pizza on a paper plate.

I bit into it and the cheese pulled away in a thread. It was so delicious I wanted to savor every bite. I watched Alexandros fold his and eat it like a sandwich in typical New York style.

Teddy continued on about his girlfriend, then pulled up a

picture on his phone to show Alexandros.

"Yea, she looks like a wild one," Alexandros said, then looked at me. "Show it to Erin. She's a good judge of character."

Teddy held up the photo to reveal an attractive, dark-haired woman with a sly grin. She was in her mid- to late thirties. "What do you think?" he asked.

I studied the photo. "I'm sure the sex is good."

Alexandros laughed.

I said, "I'm not getting that commitment is her strong suit, though. That's just the vibe I'm getting."

Teddy looked at the picture as if checking to see that same thing. He had been telling Alexandros for 20 minutes that he didn't think she was faithful, but wanted to believe the opposite was true.

The subject drifted to other things. From the corner of my eye, I saw Teddy's girlfriend crossing the street. As Teddy reached his hand out to grab hers, she ran her fingers through Alexandros's hair.

I never felt such a surge of anger and jealousy before in my life. In my head, I was lunging at her like a cat, ripping her away from him.

He flinched, which made me calm down.

Teddy put his arm around her waist and pulled her toward him. She removed her hand, but my blood was still boiling.

"Do you want to go?" I asked Alexandros, unsure if I could sit there any longer.

"Do you?" he said.

"Yes," I said.

He stood up, saying good-bye to his friends, announcing his phone number out loud. For a brief moment I thought he did that so Teddy's girlfriend would call him.

We walked to the subway and he apologized for what happened.

"I could see the pain on your face, Erin," he said.

I admitted I hated how her actions made me feel. He liked how jealous I was. That troubled me. I didn't want to feel jealous. I wanted to feel secure in our relationship.

He took my carry-on bag by the handle and pulled it for me. That was a nice gesture.

I had debated staying with Clay, but Alexandros said he wanted me there Friday night so I had agreed. I knew it was a bad idea.

When we stepped off the 7 train to wait for the E, the sun had set. He'd put my bag down and I leaned it up against the bench between the tracks and smiled. I was more content at that moment than I have ever been, yet at precisely that moment it was all kicked out from under me.

A quiet darkness filled the sky. Then I had an eerie feeling. Nobody was around. I noticed Alexandros looking at me. He was studying me, trying to predict my reaction to what he was about to say.

"Erin, I have to ask you something."

"Okay," I said. "Is it bad?"

"No. Well, not really," he said.

That relieved me. "Okay, what is it?" I asked.

"Can I borrow some money?"

My heart sank; I was so confused. That had been the last thing I had expected him to say. I had spent so much money on this trip to see him. His words hurt. I didn't know how to express that to him without knowing there was going to be an argument and ruining what I had thought was a perfect afternoon with him.

I recalled his constant bouts with his mom and sister. The arguments seemed to hinge on him asking for money and them often refusing. I couldn't figure out why he would've went out of his way to buy everything for me that day, only to turn around and ask for money later. It didn't make sense.

I turned to the night sky and asked my old friend, New York, for help silently. I looked at the Empire State Building and shrugged my shoulders. I had my back to him.

"Does that upset you?" he asked. There was an edge in his voice I'd never noticed before and for the first time I felt afraid of him. I knew he had a temper, but he had never shown it to me. I hesitated before I answered. I was talking to a ticking bomb that could explode at any moment.

I softened my voice and said, "I just spent $300 on a ticket to come here to see you. I don't have a lot of extra money with me."

If he could've shot fire from his eyes I would've been a charred marshmallow.

"Thanks for throwing *that* in my face," he huffed, turning away from me.

I was stunned and didn't know how to respond. Just then the train pulled up.

He walked on ahead of me, muttering under his breath how I was treating him the same way his mom and sister did.

I sat down next to him, but he wouldn't look at me. I could see he was enraged. I mimed pulling a knife out of my chest and throwing it on the subway floor. It didn't get a reaction from him. Instead, he kept his face turned away from me.

Now what? Should I get off at the next stop and go to Clay's? Was he going to stay this upset at me the entire visit? Our perfect day was crumbling around us.

I leaned toward him. "Look, I'm sorry, but I can't help how I feel." I wasn't even sure why *I* was apologizing.

He didn't respond.

We stepped off the E train and onto the F, which would take us to his neighborhood. We stood facing each other when Alexandros pulled up a picture of me on his phone. It was the only semi-dirty picture I had ever sent him. It was of me wearing a sweater revealing tons of cleavage.

He held it up in front of my face. "Look at that," he said.

A man next to us craned his head, looking at it.

"Put that away," I said.

Alexandros started laughing.

He felt like a stranger to me. *Who was this guy?* This was a side of him I'd never seen.

We made it to his house. I tried to ease the tension. I said, "Okay, so we just had our first fight."

"That wasn't a fight," he said in a tone that made me wonder what he considered an argument.

His apartment was in the basement of a house. It was small with a low ceiling. The pipes were in plain sight overhead and I could feel myself fighting a claustrophobic attack. We sat down on his bed and he said he was going to order us dinner.

Again, the request for money was confusing me. Dinner came, and he placed a paper plate in front of me. He said he was going to feed me like a queen. He was proud to be able to treat me and I appreciated that he was making an effort.

We ate and watched TV. Later we kissed, but this kiss felt different. It was as if our love bubble had popped. I wasn't sure why or how.

There was a disconnect that had never been there before. I wasn't sure if it was with me or him, or both of us.

I was used to him calling me my name in Greek and holding me after we made love. Instead, he took my pillow, rolled over, and fell asleep - how romantic. Clearly, something had changed. That gut feeling I had before I left home was becoming more and more accurate.

I couldn't sleep that night. I didn't feel safe sleeping next to him. Much like I had felt while waiting for the train, I was afraid of him.

In the early morning hours, I could've sworn he rolled over and elbowed me. I thought it had happened while he was sleeping, but in the morning when we were both fully awake he apologized for it. The edge returned in his voice and made me feel as if he didn't want me there.

I picked up my things and went in the bathroom and showered, wondering how I'd never seen this side of him before. It dawned on me that all the times he kept me at bay was him working very hard to hide the Mr. Hyde part of his personality. I had clearly ignored all the signs. He was becoming less and less attractive by the minute.

The next day he walked me to the subway. I saw another display of uncontrollable anger when someone bumped into him in passing. I thought he was going to kill the guy.

As we waited for the Long Island Railroad to arrive and take me to Penn Station I knew this would probably be the last time I would ever see Alexandros. I tried to hug him as I said good-bye, but he got angry when I touched him.

I told him I loved him in Greek. He didn't respond.

The train pulled up and I waited for the doors to open.

Alexandros started to leave, when, much to my surprise, he stopped and turned around.

I wanted to run and hug him one last time, but there was now a wall between us. Before I got on the train, my eyes met his and he said what he always said to me.

"You look good, Erin."

I smiled even as my heart was breaking. I knew it would be a long time before I'd see the Greek lion again, if ever.

I sat down on the LIRR and sunk down in my seat, tears

streaming down my face. *What had happened between us?*

When I got off the train in Penn Station I told myself to put him out of my mind and enjoy the rest of my time in New York. I made my way out into Times Square and headed to the Dramatist Guild to meet Clay. As soon as I saw him, Clay said something that made me laugh uncontrollably. Thank God for his humor.

We went to dinner and I explained to Clay what had happened with Alexandros. He didn't seem to know what to make of it.

"Are you going to see him again?"

"We're supposed to see each other tomorrow or Sunday, but I doubt it. I'm not sure I want to."

"Just give him a day to calm down," Clay said.

We went to Clay's gym together later that night and ran next to each other on an elliptical, making each other laugh the entire time. The laughter helped, at least for a little while.

The next day I went to Queens to see Soyhun and her new baby. I had no idea what to expect when Soyhun opened the door. She and her husband looked as if they hadn't slept in weeks, and I'm guessing they probably hadn't. Soyhun had on a T-shirt and sweat pants and a baby doughnut wrapped around her waist. She confessed she hadn't showered in two days and probably smelled like breast milk. I told her there was no need to apologize.

I looked at her baby boy lying on their bed, moving and squirming. He was so angelic, so perfect with lots of hair. I went to the bed and sat quietly next to him.

  Dorothy Never Got Down Like This

"He'll start to cry. Just wait," Soyhun said, and as if on cue, he began to squawk.

Soyhun asked me to bring him to her.

I picked him up and brought him into the living room.

She lifted up her shirt and began to feed him. She said she was having trouble feeding him and I could tell she was frustrated.

As I watched her struggle, I felt guilty. I had wondered why she didn't want to work on the rewrites for *Out of the Blue*. Not having a child of my own, I had no idea how much effort it took.

She peered up at me with tired eyes. "My joints are so sore. I can barely make a fist." She put up her hand but could barely bend her fingers to her palm.

I was shocked.

She said it was a common symptom in Asian women after pregnancy. She admitted it was too difficult to play at the moment. It was painful for her. Playing piano was her livelihood.

I didn't stay long. I had been getting angry and impatient with her for weeks now when all the while she was struggling. As I took a deep breath and tried to make peace with the situation I felt my phone buzz in my pocket.

It was Alexandros. He said he'd been called into work and wouldn't be able to see me.

I thanked him for letting me know. I wondered if things might be okay after all. I only wondered it for a second because deep down inside I knew the answer to that question. It would never be the same between us.

The next day was Sunday. I went to church with Clay, Tres, and Sabrina just as I had when I still lived in Astoria. It was good to be with them again.

Afterwards, I went back to Clay's to take a nap. I had barely slept the night before. At 4 PM I got a call from Alexandros. I didn't want to answer it, but I did.

"I can't get together today," he said. "I worked twenty hours yesterday and got to bed late."

I felt like anything I said would warrant an argument as I could hear the anger in his voice. I took a deep breath. I had to respond. "What's wrong? What happened between us? What changed?"

"I haven't changed," he said curtly. "You have." Then he hung up.

I hated to admit it, but he was right.

Clay came back and I told him about the conversation.

"Well, that's what happens when you're in love. You change," he said.

Clay was right. I loved Alexandros. I suspected I always would.

At the airport the next morning I stood waiting to get on the plane. I felt sick. Everything I had worked so hard for in New York was gone. My relationship was over. Soyhun had moved on with her life. We hadn't heard from our director. I stood there knowing that I was standing on the platform waiting for Professor Marvel and his hot air balloon all by myself. My Scarecrow wasn't with me. There was no Tin Man in my story and my Lion had turned out to be cowardly after all.

I stared at the gate about to board, wondering how I was going to make it through the flight without throwing up or crying. My time in Oz was over.

As I sat down in my seat on the plane my phone buzzed. I looked, curious. It was a text from Alexandros.

Have a good trip back, Erin.

I turned off my phone. What was the point of this text now? I didn't want to take the flight back to Wisconsin. I wanted to click my heels together and be back there, without a flight in between and without the pain and disappointment I somehow knew I was going to suffer even before I left Wisconsin.

I was sitting next to a woman who started to talk to me a few minutes into the flight. She had traveled all over the world and lived in Milwaukee. She was so interesting that she took my mind off of all that had happened. She asked me where I would want to go if I could go anywhere. I told her I wanted to see Ireland someday.

"You know, Erin, you can start saving money now, and in a few months, you'll be able to go on a trip."

I wondered if that would be my next adventure.

I pondered her suggestion for a long moment. Wherever I went from now on, I would do it fearlessly. After my move to New York, I was so much braver and more confident and maybe that was the reason for that adventure.

When the plane landed, I thanked her for the conversation.

As I stepped out into the quiet, familiar surroundings of Milwaukee's General Mitchell airport I felt a sense of calm come over me. I remembered all the times I had waited in that airport. Waiting to fly to New York, waiting to meet Soyhun, waiting to see the man I loved. Waiting, waiting, waiting… Yet Wisconsin was always there for me. It was there all along, my home. I checked in with my heart and it said *stay*.

I had certainly learned that the hard way in my many journeys to and from New York. I hadn't given up on my dream. I had seen it through. I was done chasing it. And now I didn't need to wonder what would've happened if I had never tried? I knew, and I was grateful for the journey.

Epilogue

There's No Place Like Home

Sometime in the future

Just as Dorothy woke up from her dream, I woke up back in Wisconsin after my New York City adventure, but this time I was grateful for the Dairy State. I was grateful for every New York moment I had, but also the perspective I had returning. This story isn't over yet though. Just when I thought would end up writing the end with a simple 'it's not the destination, it's the journey,' which I still believe to be true, a new ending emerged – one that seems the most fitting for my story.

First – the love story. Well, let's be real, it wasn't much of one. I stopped looking for Mr. Right and in that time, gained some perspective on just how deserving I was of real love and what that looked like to me. Then, as luck would happen, I met the man I am going to marry, and I met him, oddly enough, in Wisconsin. I never expected to find that, in fact I had given up on it all together and was completely at peace with my life just as it was, when he showed up. I don't want to share too many details – that's another book entirely, but instead, I want to say that the biggest thing I learned was not to chase someone who doesn't want to be caught. Alexandros wasn't ready and frankly neither was I. I will always think fondly of him and remember him as a character who made my NYC life interesting. I hope he's well. The last time I talked to him was pre-pandemic (COVID-19, 2020).

While back in Wisconsin, I've had the pleasure of teaching theatre at a local college, writing and performing stand-up comedy and starting my own publishing company. I am doing what I love and couldn't have done any of it without my New York experiences.

Soyun and I continued to work on Out of the Blue, when, very much 'out of the blue' we had a call from a performing arts center right here in Green Bay, Wisconsin. Just when I had put it on a shelf and began writing other things, we learned that our show will be performed there next spring. It seems very fitting it should make its debut in Green Bay where the story is set. I'm not sure if that will be the end for our musical, in fact, it may just be the beginning. Dorothy may still go to Broadway. Who knows…

I recall my Mom telling me before I moved to New York City, that I might just find everything I dreamed of right in my own backyard one day, and, much like Dorothy realizes, it was all right there all the time. I just had to come back with a new perspective to find it. It's true – there's no place like home.

About the Author

Erin Hunsader is an author, publisher, and stand-up comedian. Besides continuing to develop her writing and comedy career, she is also always on the lookout for a good story for her publishing company, Penbird Press LLC. Her musical, *OUT OF THE BLUE*, co-written with composer, Haesun Suh was selected for World Premiere Wisconsin and is currently in development. She continues to perform her play, *Monologues from Dead Celebrities* (co-written with Jeremy Pelegrin) along with trying to master the violin (or just play it without her cats covering their ears.) She resides in Appleton, WI.

9 789898 504190 3